D0577142

Quest for the Cup

Quest for

A HISTORY OF THE STANLEY CUP FINALS 1893–2001

GENERAL EDITOR: JACK FALLA

Jack Batten, Lance Hornby,

George Johnson, Steve Milton

KEY PORTER BOOKS

the Cup

Hockey Hall of Fame: 1, 3 (Doug MacLellan), 10 (Doug MacLellan), 11, 12, 13, 14, 15, 16, 18, 19, 20, 21, 22, 23, 24 (James Rice), 25 (top, James Rice), 26,28, 29, 32 (James Rice), 34, 36, 37 (left, James Rice), 38, 39, 41, 42, 43, 44, 45, 46, 47, 48-49, 50, 51 (James Rice), 52 (upper and lower right, Imperial Oil-Turofsky), 53 (upper and lower right, Imperial Oil-Turofsky), 54, 55, 56, 57, 58, 59, 60, 61, 62, 63, 64, 65 (lower, Imperial Oil-Turofsky), 66, 67 (left, Imperial Oil-Turofsky), 69 (Imperial Oil-Turofsky), 70, 71 (Imperial Oil-Turofsky), 72 (Imperial Oil-Turofsky), 76 (upper and lower, Imperial Oil-Turofsky), 77 (Imperial Oil-Turofsky), 78-79 (Imperial Oil-Turofsky), 80, 81(Imperial Oil-Turofsky), 82 (Imperial Oil-Turofsky), 83 (Imperial Oil-Turofsky), 84 (Imperial Oil-Turofsky), 85 (Imperial Oil-Turofsky), 86-87 (Imperial Oil-Turofsky), 88 (Imperial Oil-Turofsky), 89 (Imperial Oil-Turofsky), 90 (Imperial Oil-Turofsky), 92 (Imperial Oil-Turofsky), 93 (Imperial Oil-Turofsky), 94 (Imperial Oil-Turofsky), 97 (Frank Prazac), 98 (Graphic Artists), 99 (Imperial Oil-Turofsky), 100 (left, Imperial Oil-Turofsky), 101 (Imperial Oil-Turofsky), 102 (Imperial Oil-Turofsky), 105 (Frank Prazac), 106-107 (Imperial Oil-Turofsky), 108 (Imperial Oil-Turofsky), 110 (Imperial Oil-Turofsky), 111, 112 (upper, Graphic Artists)113, 114-115 (Imperial Oil-Turofsky), 116 (Imperial Oil-Turofsky), 117 (Imperial Oil-Turofsky), 118 (Frank Prazac), 119 (Imperial Oil-Turofsky), 125 (Frank Prazac), 126 (Frank Prazac), 127 (Graphic Artists), 128 (Frank Prazac), 129 (Frank Prazac), 131, 132 (London Life-Portnoy), 133 (Frank Prazac), 134 (Frank Prazac), 140, 144 (London Life-Portnoy), 148 (Graphic Artists), 149 (lower, London Life-Portnoy), 282 (lower right, Imperial Oil-Turofsky), 283 (right), 284 (lower left (Imperial Oil-Turofsky) and right), 285(Graphic Artists).

Bruce Bennett Studios: 17, 30, 31, 74, 91, 104, 120, 121, 122-123, 124, 131, 136, 138-139, 142, 143, 145, 146, 147, 149 (top), 151, 153, 154, 155, 156, 158-159, 160, 161, 162-163, 164, 165, 166, 167, 168, 169, 170, 171, 172-173, 174, 176, 177, 178-179, 180, 181, 182-183, 184, 186, 187, 188, 189, 191, 192, 194-195, 196-197, 198-199, 200, 202, 203, 204, 205, 206-207, 208-209, 210, 211, 212-213, 214, 215, 217, 218-219, 220, 222, 224, 225, 226, 227, 228, 230, 231, 232, 233, 234-235, 236, 237, 238, 242, 243, 244-245, 246, 247, 248-249, 250, 251, 282 (top), 284 (top), 286, 287,288, 289, 290, 291, 292, 293, 294, 295, 296 (left).

Canadian Press Archives: 130, 152, 240-241, 252, 253, 254, 255, 256-257, 258, 259, 260, 261, 262, 263, 264-265, 266, 267, 268, 269, 270, 271, 272, 273, 274, 275, 276, 277, 278, 279, 280, 281, 283 (left), 284, 296 (right), 297.

National Library of Canada Cataloguing in Publication Data

Quest for the Cup : a history of the Stanley cup finals 1893-2001

Includes index
ISBN: 1-55263-343-8

1. Stanley Cup (Hockey)–History. I. Falla, Jack, 1944-
II. Johnson, George (George Jonas), 1957–
QV847.7.Q48 2001 796.962'648 C2001-900593-8

The publisher gratefully acknowledges the support of the Canada Council for the Arts and the Ontario Arts Council for its publishing program.

Canadä

We acknowledge the financial support of the Government of Canada through the Book Publishing Industry Development Program (BPIDP) for our publishing activities.

Key Porter Books Limited
70 The Esplanade
Toronto, Ontario
Canada M5E 1R2

www.keyporter.com

Cover design: Peter Maher
Electronic formatting: Jean Lightfoot Peters

Printed and bound in Spain

01 02 03 04 05 06 6 5 4 3 2 1

Lord Stanley of Preston, founder of the Stanley Cup.

Contents

Introduction: An "Outward and Visible Sign"

The Stanley Cup defines careers. "I want to kiss the Cup," Montreal rookie Rejean Houle said so many times during Montreal's 1971 Cup run that the phrase became a kind of team mantra, giving collective voice to the dream of everyone who has played the game in North America. Hoisting the Cup, kissing it, drinking from it, taking it home for a day with family and friends marks the supreme moment in a player's career.

At the threshold of retirement, a reminiscent Wayne Gretzky said simply that winning his first Cup with Edmonton in 1984 was, "my sweetest moment in hockey."

"Lifting that Cup is the best memory I have of the game," said Pittsburgh's Mario Lemieux.

Jean Beliveau, who played on ten Cup-winning teams in Montreal, still calls his first Cup win his biggest thrill in hockey. It is a sentiment echoed in only slightly different words by virtually every player on every Cup-winning team.

So meaningful and symbolic is the Stanley Cup that during a team party at Henri Richard's Tavern following Montreal's 1979 victory, Guy Lafleur slipped out of the party with the Cup and drove to his parents' home in Thurso, Quebec, to put the trophy on the lawn of his childhood home—the same lawn on which his father had built the makeshift rink on which five-year-old Guy had acquired his speed and intuitive comprehension of the game. While the Canadiens officially "reprimanded" Lafleur for the spontaneous heist, it was only a few years later that the NHL began to allow each member of a Cup-winning team to take the trophy home for a day to share with family and friends.

A Cup win can also be a defining moment in the life of a fan. Few of us who saw it will forget the handmade sign held aloft by a Rangers fan in New York's Madison Square Garden on June 14, 1994 as the final horn sounded on New York's first Cup win since 1940. "Now I Can Die Happy," the sign read.

But if winning the Cup defines a career or a team, the same goes, sadly, for *not* winning it. In March of 2000, then thirty-nine-year old Boston defenseman Raymond Bourque—one of the game's all-time greats and heir to the mantle of Eddie Shore and Bobby Orr as living

symbols of this Original Six franchise—asked to be traded to a team that had a realistic chance of winning the Cup. When he finally won the Cup with Colorado's victory over New Jersey on June 9, 2001, Bourque was smiling through a tear-streaked face as he hoisted and kissed the trophy and shouts of "Ray...Ray...Ray" rained down from the stands. "It eluded me for so long," he said, "It's so great to be able to say 'Yes, I've won one.'"

When, in 1892, British nobleman Sir Frederick Arthur Stanley, Baron Stanley of Preston and Governor General of Canada, donated the Stanley Cup, he wrote that he intended the trophy to be an "outward and visible sign" of an annual championship held among the best hockey teams in Canada. The Cup—surely one of the most recognizable trophies in the world (for instance, do you know what trophy for the World Series looks like?)—exceeded even that lordly intention on the night of May 18, 1971 in Chicago Stadium. It was minutes after the Canadiens had beaten the Black Hawks in the seventh game of the final that Montreal captain Jean Beliveau, having just played the last game of his twenty-year career, raised the Stanley Cup above his head and led a slow parade around the rink. While captains of winning teams had raised the Cup before and, in 1970, Bruins captain Johnny Bucyk was virtually chased around the Boston Garden ice by jubilant fans, there had been nothing as stately and deliberate as Beliveau's gesture, the meaning of which was gracefully captured by legendary sportswriter Herbert Warren Wind. Reporting in *The New Yorker* magazine, Wind wrote that fans "perceived almost instantly that they were looking at no conquering foe but at a rare gentleman whose manner as he displayed the Cup said, 'I am not merely celebrating the Canadiens' triumph. I am celebrating the superb game of ice hockey and what it means to all of us.'" Beliveau brought a whole new meaning to the ceremony, and since that time the circling of the rink with the huge trophy held aloft has come to be regarded as the perfect climax to the long season.

My fellow writers Jack Batten, Lance Hornby, George Johnson and Steve Milton, along with the photographers, designers and editors whose work makes up this book, hope that *Quest for the Cup* will, like the trophy itself, celebrate "the superb game of ice hockey and what it means to all of us."

Ultimately, the Stanley Cup is important because it connects us to the game we love—and, thus, to each other.

JACK FALLA

A Modest Investment in Dreams 1893–1926

Lord Stanley bought the Cup for 10 British guineas, or roughly $50.

The images that remain to us a century or so later—dog-eared sepia photographs of earnest young men looking sporting in a college sort of way, sticks crossed in front of them, standing in front of bowler-hatted, high-collared team executives with thick handlebar mustaches—not only seem, when studied today, from another time and another place, they could be from another planet.

This was the dawn of the Stanley Cup, the years before the National Hockey League (NHL) took hockey's greatest prize as its personal property. A time when amateurs from across the country and beyond, from Edmonton and Saskatoon and Regina and, yes, even Seattle, had an opportunity to lift, to embrace, what would in time become hockey's holy grail the world over. A system in which the Cup could be challenged for by simply notifying a pair of league trustees. A moment in time when a dollar got you a reserved seat in any arena.

The years 1893 to 1926 were an era of legendary talents, many of whose names continue to resonate for those who love the game. Of Art Ross. And Lester Patrick. Of Newsy Lalonde. And Cyclone Taylor. Of Frank McGee. And Georges Vezina. Those names, their legacies, are engraved in the base of the silver bowl they all still play for; all still dream about. The tapestry was rich, innovative and, if you shake away the cobwebs, dust off the old newspaper clippings and give in to the rosy hue of nostalgia, no less than unforgettable.

The Stanley Cup, of course, is one of the oldest, most prestigious and certainly most

recognizable trophies in North America, a glittering star in the sporting constellation. It is precisely this age, that history, those indelible men and their deeds that has down through the years made the winning all the sweeter. From Richard to Howe, from Hull to Lafleur, from Gretzky to Lemieux, when they've held the Stanley Cup on the ice in victory, their eyes have scanned the many rings of

The Montreal AAA were the first team to win the Stanley Cup, in 1893, and the first and last to turn it down.

There was no controversy surrounding Montreal's second Cup win in 1894.

The Winnipeg Vics in 1895. They would become champions in the next season.

the rickety silver mug and realized the weight not only in pounds, but in tears, in sweat, in passion. The formative years of the Stanley Cup teem with intriguing stories. As with any venture in its infancy, there was trial and error, success and failure.

In 1896, for instance, Winnipeg goalie G. H. Merritt stole the Stanley Cup thunder from eventual champions Montreal by donning white cricket pads to block pucks, which immediately became all the rage. Until 1916, the two defense positions were referred to as point and coverpoint, the former maintaining close proximity to the goalkeeper, the latter moving up into the rush, à la Paul Coffey.

Think Mike Keenan and Scotty Bowman get a tad testy over questionable calls? Between 1893 and the turn of the century, nets consisted of two flagged posts embedded in the ice and an imaginary crossbar. No goal line. No netting. Certainly fans in the majority of buildings are a rabid bunch these days. But even the rowdy Madison Square Garden crowd had nothing on irate Quebec fans during the 1895 season. Well before a structured playoff format had been instituted to decide an ultimate champion, a particularly heated Quebec-Ottawa game ended with the referee being dragged back to the arena (he'd fled following the final whistle), where the mob tried to persuade him to call the game a tie, Ottawa's 3–2 win having sparked the near-riot. Police eventually were summoned and the presiding official, a Mr. Hamilton by name, was rescued. Quebec, meanwhile, was subsequently suspended for the remainder of the season.

Players today constantly complain about shoddy ice conditions in arenas, and with the quick, constant turnovers from cement to ice and back again to accommodate the heavy volume of events in many buildings, it can get a bit rough. Well, gentlemen, count your blessings. When the Rat Portage (Kenora) Westerners first challenged Ottawa for the Cup in March 1903, the ice conditions were so abysmal reports insist that on one occasion the puck fell through a hole in the ice and vanished, never to be seen again.

The Montreal Victorias' 1897 Stanley Cup–winning side.

The first three decades of Cup competition saw the shift from strictly amateurs to a mix of amateurs and professionals to strictly pros. Teams from seventeen different leagues were declared champions. The era heralded the expansion to large U.S. markets. It gave us the original Montreal Forum. It introduced the National Hockey League, which formed in 1918 after some quarreling among directors of the National Hockey Association (NHA). It provided the launching pad for all that was to come. And all that is yet to be.

This mostly glorious, sometimes comical, often unbelievable saga started, of all things, with a politician's love for the game. Or rather, the love of his sons. Lord Stanley of Preston, the sixth Governor General of Canada, instituted a perpetual challenge trophy to be contested for the amateur hockey championship, apparently because his two boys, Arthur and Algernon, enjoyed pulling on their skates and playing on Ottawa's Rideau Canal. The boys' interest sparked the building of a large outdoor rink at Rideau Hall and an award for the finest hockey team in Canada. The Stanley Cup was originally called the Dominion Hockey Challenge Cup but quickly became known by the name of the man who ordered it made and shipped from England. The early recipients of the Stanley Cup actually were required to post a bond to make sure the trophy was returned safe and sound to the trustees. And winners had to pay to have their names engraved on its base.

The Stanley Cup hauled out to center ice for victory celebrations today isn't the heirloom donated by Lord Stanley, of course. Over the years, bands, or "collars," of silver were added to the bowl and base to keep up with the increasing number of champions. By the early 1960s, metallurgists warned the Cup had become too brittle and might shatter if dropped. So the original bowl was taken off the base in 1967, and three years later a Montreal silversmith painstakingly copied the bowl down to scratches and teeth marks left by overzealous winners. A safe haven was found for the original Stanley Cup in the Hockey Hall of Fame in Toronto. So while there might have been some grumbling in the mid-to-late 1890s about the engraving outlay, the pittance they were asked to ante up turned out to be well worth the investment. Their names are on there still, in plain sight, for eternity.

It's only fitting, of course, that a team from Montreal, known as the Montreal Amateur Athletic Association (AAA), would be the first recipient of the Cup (which at that time resembled a fair-sized holiday punch bowl), heading the five-team Amateur Hockey Association standings with a 7–1 record in 1892–93. Twenty games were contested that first season, with three entries from the city of Montreal—the Victorias, the Crystals and Montreal AAA—as well as teams from Quebec and Ottawa. Haviland Routh was hailed as the undisputed star of the winners, the first scoring ace on record, hitting for twelve goals. What followed has gone down in hockey lore as "The Snub."

When the Montreal Amateur Athletic Association's executive went to present the Cup to the players, they turned it down! Didn't want it. Theories abound as to why. Perhaps the team didn't feel it was worth the effort to collect such a new trophy. Another explanation had the team upset at not being invited to the Cup presentation proper (the executive was formally given the Cup—not the players). Whatever. The MAAA would win the Cup again in 1894, this time with no post-championship controversies, before the crosstown Victorias began a storied run of success. Routh, who scored an unheard-of five goals in the season-opening rout of rival Quebec, would lead Montreal to the back-to-back titles, the 1894 season notable for Quebec pulling out over a rancorous dispute about where the final should in fact be staged. That season, owing to a four-way tie atop the league standings, marked the first form of

Cricket, anyone? Winnipeg goalie G. H. Merritt's white cricket pads became all the rage.

Stanley Cup playoff games. Ironic, because by-now retired Lord Stanley had returned to England and never actually saw one contested.

In 1895, the Montreal Victorias were crowned the Amateur Hockey Association champions. However, the Cup trustees had already accepted a challenge by Queen's University to play the Montreal AAA (the 1894 champs). It was decided that if Queen's defeated the Montreal AAA, they would be declared winners of the Stanley Cup. If the Montreal AAA won, the Montreal Victorias would claim the coveted chalice. On March 9, 1895, the Montreal AAA pounded the university team 5–1, allowing the Montreal Victorias to lay claim to the Cup.

The 1896 season had an interesting twist, in that two clubs—the Montreal Vics and Winnipeg Victorias—were declared Stanley Cup champions within the calendar year. Winnipeg, with Merritt decked out in his trendsetting white cricket pads, had challenged the eastern Vics in February and wound up knocking them right off in Montreal 2–0. But a rematch ten months later in the Manitoba capital provided a different outcome, Montreal gaining revenge in a thrilling 6–5 shootout. The eastern Vics would win again in 1897 and then in 1898, marking them as the first Stanley Cup dynasty. In coverpoint Mike Grant, a former junior speed-skating star, the Vics were fortunate enough to have on their roster the Bobby Orr of his time. By all reports, Grant was a solid defender and

The final and most powerful of the Montreal Vics' four-Cup dynasty, 1898.

The Montreal Shamrocks ended their crosstown rivals' reign in 1899.

The legendary Ottawa Silver Seven of 1905 easily repelled the Cup's most bizarre challenge—made by a team from Dawson City, Yukon.

Dickie Boon, one of Montreal's "Little Men of Iron."

mesmerizing when carrying the puck, with an unparalleled combination of speed and savvy.

Perhaps the most well-rounded of the four Vics' championship sides was the 1898 squad, so powerful that no one even bothered to put in a challenge to the likes of goaltender Frank Richardson and forwards Cam Davidson, Bob McDougall and captain Graham Drinkwater, who would be inducted into the Hockey Hall of Fame in 1950. The Vics' dominance ended in March 1899, when the Cup was passed to the Montreal Shamrocks as winners of the Canadian Amateur Hockey League. But the proud Victorias had defended their title admirably in February 1899 against a highly talented Winnipeg team.

This confrontation remains memorable for the second game—Montreal having taken the opener 2–1—when a particularly savage slash by McDougall to the right leg of Winnipeg rover Tony Gingras ignited an already tense situation. The Vics were leading 3–2 and little time remained in regulation. Gingras crumpled to the ice and the westerners howled to referee Jack Findlay in protest. Findlay issued McDougall nothing more than a minor penalty, incensing the Winnipeggers even further. Perhaps feeling his authority had been questioned, a miffed Findlay then left the ice, took off his skates and exited the building! It took officials fifteen minutes to find Findlay and even more time to convince him to return. By then, many of the Winnipeg players had left, as well, and the returning Findlay then announced they had fifteen minutes to put a representative product on the ice. Alas, the Winnipeg boys were even harder to locate than Findlay had been. Thus, the game was terminated and the Cup awarded to the Vics.

By 1900, the Vics were no longer a power—in fact, no longer even competitive, finishing the year with a 2–6 record. But it had been, by any measuring stick, a wonderful run. The Shamrocks, winners in March 1899, repeated in 1900. By virtue of a 7–0–1 record, Ottawa clinched the league championship in 1901, but then the Winnipeg Vics defeated the two-time Cup champion Shamrocks and it was too late to put in a challenge bid for the Cup. In that final, Winnipeg slid past the Shamrocks in an edgy two-game series, 4–3 and 2–1, ending their reign.

The 1902 bragging rights went to the Montreal AAA, the so-called "Little Men of Iron," who bested Winnipeg in a three-game March series, winning the deciding match 2–1. The "Little Men of Iron" nickname was hung on the team by newsman Peter Spanjaardt during his rinkside telegraphic play-by-play, as the much smaller AAA clung grimly to a slender lead as the minutes rolled on. The next three years, 1903 to 1905, would be dominated by the legendary Ottawa Silver Seven.

One of the greatest teams ever assembled, the Silver Seven answered the clarion call in 1905 of one of the most baffling challenges ever made, by a team from the Yukon, Northwest Territories. The Nuggets, as the band of unknown upstarts was known, were the brainchild of Toronto-born prospector Joe Boyle. Boyle had struck it filthy rich in the Yukon gold rush of 1898. The underdogs traveled over 4,000 miles to reach the Canadian capital, partway by dogsled, and paid out $3,000 for the privilege, a tremendous sum for the time, only to be annihilated 9–2 and 23–2.

Mario Lemieux and Wayne Gretzky are two modern superstars who understand the Cup's value, in terms of sweat, tears and passion.

The 1906 Montreal Wanderers prevailed 12–10 in a two-game aggregate over Ottawa in one of the most thrilling finals on record.

The second dismantling was a game in which the preeminent scoring star of the day, "One-Eyed" Frank McGee, scored an almost obscene fourteen times.

In the Cup final that season, the Silver Seven survived a first-game loss to Rat Portage to take the final two contests 4–2 and 5–4, with McGee breaking a 4–4 tie, and lay claim to their third consecutive Stanley Cup. The Ottawa-born McGee was indisputably one of the most dynamic individual stars of the age, despite losing

The Kenora Thistles briefly held the Cup in 1907 before the Wanderers took it back again.

Scoring star Art Ross of the Wanderers.

an eye through an errant high stick during an exhibition game in 1902. He would play with the Silver Seven until 1906 before retiring. When World War I broke out, McGee enlisted and was killed in action at the Battle of the Somme in 1916. In only forty-five total appearances, Frank McGee would score an impossible 134 goals, splendid by even Lemieux or Gretzky standards.

One of the era's most galvanizing talents, Newsy Lalonde, also made news in 1905, breaking in with Cornwall of the Federal League. Unfortunately, Lalonde would sever an artery during his first game and miss almost the entire season. The next year's Cup finale in March 1906 belonged to the soon-to-be-legendary player, coach and manager Lester Patrick. Patrick, playing rover, had jumped ship from the west coast to join the Montreal Wanderers that season, and the defection paid off handsomely for both he and the team.

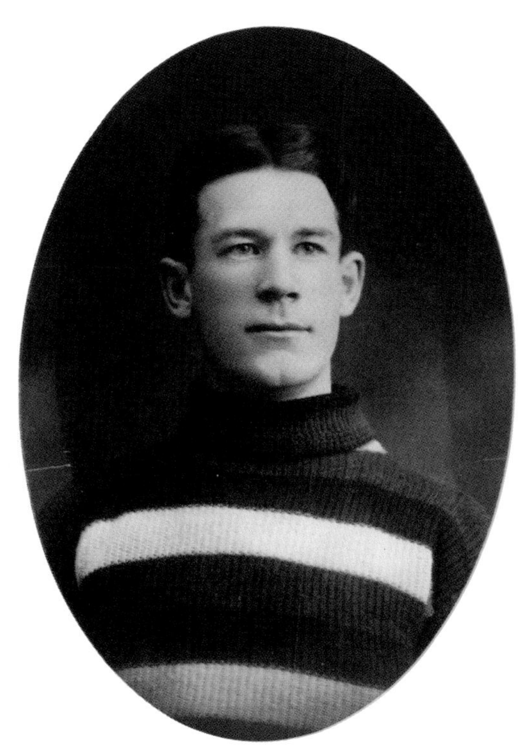

Tom Phillips in Ottawa Senators' regalia in 1907.

Cece Blatchford of the Montreal Wanderers in 1910, the year professionalism took over the game.

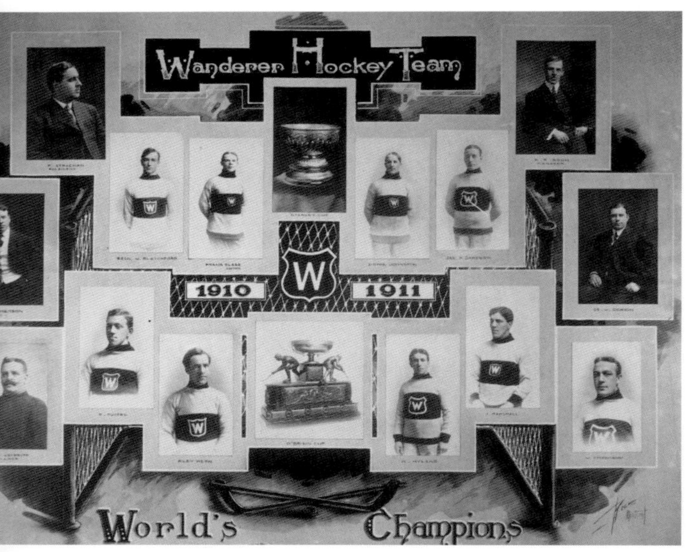

A team photograph, made up of player cards, of the 1910–11 Cup-champion Montreal Wanderers.

In one of the most astounding Cup results to that period in time, the Wanderers, opening up the two-game, total-goal finale at home, gutted the overwhelming favorites from Ottawa 9–1, paced by Ernie Russell's four goals, three from Pud Glass and the flash and dash of the ever-present Patrick. The favored Silver Seven were by consensus regarded as finished, their confidence and poise shattered by the pounding. Still, a boisterous crowd of five-thousand showed up in the Canadian capital to witness the rematch, praying for a miracle, and very nearly witnessed one.

As so often happens when a team enters a game too relaxed, too sure of itself, the Wanderers had decided sit back and defend, confident their eight-goal lead was insurmountable. And their cockiness only heightened when Ernie Johnson danced through the Ottawa defense ridiculously early in Game Two to put Montreal ahead 1–0 in the game and 10–1 in the series. The smiles and smirks were short-lived.

Throwing all caution to the wind, the Silver Seven marched forward, relentless wave after relentless wave, showing the tenacity and resilience that had helped them dominate the game for three seasons. With the Smith brothers, Harry and Alf, running amok, the Silver Seven began to dig into the deficit, at first superficially and then tellingly: 10–2, 10–3, 10–4, 10–5, 10–6, 10–7, 10–8, 10–9! Amazingly, incredibly, miraculously, when Harry Smith victimized the Wanderers for his fifth goal of the evening with ten minutes remaining, the score stood 9–1 for Ottawa and the series was all square.

Such was the pandemonium that the Governor General of Canada, caught up in the euphoria, reached over the boards to shake hands with Smith. Now it was Montreal's turn to locate some inner reserve of resolve as Ottawa, infused with new energy, continued to press forward. And, in yet another twist to an ever-changing story line, Patrick took it upon himself to turn the tide once more.

Igniting a Montreal resurgence with a few of the spectacular solo rushes he'd become famous for, Patrick put a halt to the Ottawa celebrations by scoring once, then twice. At the end, the visitors were hanging on grimly. The Silver Seven had won the game 9–3, but thanks to the sensational import from out west, the Wanderers had claimed the Stanley Cup by a 12–10 aggregate.

The Westerners, now known as the Kenora Thistles, challenged the Cup champion Wanderers in 1907, although the challenge was actually issued the previous year. Using a ringer, Art Ross, who'd been "borrowed" from Brandon, and thanks mainly to left winger Tom Phillips, who scored seven goals in two games, the Thistles prevailed 4–2 and 8–6.

Two months later, the teams met again with the Cup at stake. Immediately, the Wanderers filed a protest regarding the eligibility of Ross. Even while this was taking place, Kenora had tempted Harry Westwick and Alf Smith of Ottawa to join them for the Montreal showdown. Acting Cup trustee William Foran ruled that Westwick and Smith could not participate. Having already traveled west, however, and with Kenora steadfast in its stance to use the two imports, the Wanderers relented, withdrawing their protest, and won the two-game set anyway, on the strength of a 7–2 mauling of the Thistles in the opener. The following four seasons would become a game of championship Ping-Pong for the Wanderers and Ottawa, with Montreal prevailing in 1908, Ottawa the subsequent year, the Wanderers the next, followed by a bit of Senators payback in 1911.

The year 1910 would witness radical changes to the face of hockey. The dawn of professionalism in hockey began in earnest. The first strictly pro league in Canada, the Ontario Professional League, was formed that year. Oh, some teams limped along trying to use amateur players, but they were far from competitive. Teams' management wanted to win, and the best players wanted compensation for their services. The game was irrevocably altered. A new league, the National Hockey Association, forerunner to the NHL, was formed, and franchises were awarded to the Wanderers, Renfrew, Cobalt, Haileybury and a team in Montreal to be known as the Canadiens.

With the mining business booming in Ontario, Ambrose O'Brien, owner of the Renfrew Millionaires, went on a spending spree that at the time rivaled the present-day New York Rangers. O'Brien bought Cyclone Taylor, the two Patrick brothers, Lester and Frank, and the Cleghorn boys, Sprague and Odie. This was the year that after boasting to a newspaper about being able to score a goal while skating backward, Taylor apparently did, spinning around at the end

Legend has it that Fred "Cyclone" Taylor of the Renfrew Millionaires once scored a goal while skating backwards!

One of the legendary Patrick brothers, Frank, during his stint with the Vancouver Millionaires.

When Canadiens' legendary goaltender Georges Vezina (seen here in 1920) died tragically of tuberculosis in the spring of 1926, it marked the end of an era.

of a foray up ice before beating the goaltender, during a late-season game against Ottawa. At least, so legend has it. And quoting a wonderful line from the 1960s John Ford western *The Man Who Shot Liberty Valance*, a movie about the power of myth: "When the legend becomes fact, print the legend."

Taylor, nicknamed "Cyclone" by the Governor General, Earl Grey, easily qualifies for legend status. Such was Taylor's fame at the time that he was given a $5,250 contract by O'Brien, nearly double what he was earning from the Ottawa Senators. A staggering sum of money, particularly for a twelve-game season (by comparison, "the Georgia Peach," Ty Cobb, was being paid $6,500 for a 154-game Major League Baseball season). Still, for all the money O'Brien shelled out, the Millionaires weren't a factor in the Stanley Cup chase. The Wanderers were awarded the trophy from defending titleholder Ottawa for winning the NHA championship.

In 1911, three periods of twenty minutes were instituted, rather than two periods of thirty, and one of the greatest goaltenders of all time, Georges Vezina, debuted in net for the Montreal Canadiens. His coolness under fire and his birthplace quickly earned him the nickname the "Chicoutimi Cucumber." Vezina—who, as a sideline to tending goal, fathered twenty-one children—played through sickness and injury for fifteen seasons, 328 league games and thirty-nine in the playoffs. Legend has it

Joe Malone and the Quebec Bulldogs were back-to-back champions in 1912 and 1913.

that the Canadiens were on an exhibition tour of rural Quebec, came upon the lanky local kid in the lumber town of Chicoutimi and couldn't beat him! If you can't beat 'em, sign 'em. Which is what Montreal management did. They never regretted the decision. Tragically, Vezina would die of tuberculosis in the spring of 1926.

On November 28, 1925, his illness finally manifested itself for all to see during a Canadiens game in Pittsburgh. Playing despite searing chest pains and a fever that would've put most men in hospital, Vezina felt terrible in the dressing room following the first period. Later, it would be known that he had suffered a slight hemorrhage. Undaunted, the Chicoutimi Cucumber took his place in the net. Suddenly, to the horror of the crowd and his teammates, he crumbled to the ice. The next day Vezina made one final trip to the Canadiens dressing room. He was dead four months later, far too soon, at thirty-nine years old. Vezina's name today, of course, is synonymous with the goaltender voted as the NHL's best by league general managers. Nothing could be more fitting.

The Quebec Bulldogs then put together back-to-back championships, in 1912 and 1913. In 1913, they answered a challenge bid from the Canadian Maritimes, from Sydney, Nova Scotia, whose team reminded everyone of the ill-advised Dawson City challenge of Ottawa eight years earlier. The Bulldogs paddled Sydney by a cumulative count of 20–5 in a two-game, total-goal series. In 1912, the Toronto Blueshirts, forerunners of the Maple Leafs, had been formed, fielding a solid lineup that included Harry Holmes, Jack Walker and Frank Nighbor.

Within two years, Toronto was challenging for the Cup, lining up against the powerful Canadiens. Montreal, however, was severely hampered by a separated shoulder suffered by Newsy Lalonde, who continued to play through the pain, but his usual effectiveness was greatly diminished. The Canadiens won 2–0 at home but were trashed by six goals in the rematch. Toronto subsequently accepted the offer of a two-game series from Victoria of the Pacific Coast Hockey Association (PCHA), who'd traveled east despite neglecting to put in a formal Cup bid with the trustees. The potentially explosive possibility of Victoria winning the series but not the Cup was negated, however, when the Blueshirts took both games by a single goal.

Goalie Clint Benedict starred in the Montreal Maroons' 1926 title run.

The PCHA had been the brainchild of the Patrick brothers, Lester and Frank. The Patrick name, arguably the most famous in hockey history, is still being carried on today, by Pittsburgh Penguins general manager Craig Patrick. The first Stanley Cup series played west of Winnipeg, featuring Ottawa of the NHA and the Vancouver Millionaires, champions of the Pacific Coast Hockey Association, capped the 1915 season. The Millionaires, run by Frank Patrick, were by all accounts an impressive unit, so strong in fact that when they attempted to add Lester Patrick to the roster to fill an injury void and were turned down by Ottawa, Frank Patrick merely shrugged. His apparent indifference was proven well-founded. The Millionaires laid waste to Ottawa, outscoring their rivals in the three games contested. Acquisitions Cyclone Taylor and Frank Nighbor were the stars.

After that series, the general opinion was that the hockey being played in the PCHA was far superior to that of the NHA and that the Cup would remain out west for some time to come. That general opinion turned out to be wrong. The 1916 season, in fact, not only saw a return to power by the east, but the first of twenty-four Stanley Cup victories by the Canadiens. The Canadiens even knocked off the first U.S.-based finalist in history, the Portland Rosebuds of the PCHA, but only by a 2–1 count in a fifth and deciding game. With World War I dominating people's thoughts, and many of hockey's stars now serving their country overseas, Seattle of the PCHA hauled the Cup back to the coast in 1917 by besting the Canadiens before Toronto took it back by beating Vancouver the next season.

The year 1919 will be remembered for being the only Cup final abandoned, due to an influenza epidemic that gripped the continent. The final series between Coast league champion Seattle and the Montreal Canadiens was tied two games apiece with a scoreless draw thrown in for good measure at the time. A deciding game had been set for April 1, but Joe Hall of the Canadiens was already in a hospital with a high fever. Three of his teammates, including the dynamic Newsy Lalonde, had taken to their beds at home, as well as manager George Kennedy. An offer was made to complete the series using Victoria players for the ailing Canadiens. That plan was quickly abandoned. The disappointment of not being able to

Jack Darragh played his entire career—six seasons—for the Ottawa Senators.

Cecil "Babe" Dye scored nine goals in five games for Toronto St. Pats in the 1922 final.

complete the Stanley Cup playoffs was quickly put in perspective, and turned to tragedy, when on April 5, Joe Hall died in a Seattle hospital.

Backstopped by Clint Benedict, Ottawa would place its grip on the Cup in both the 1920 and 1921 seasons, toppling Seattle in 1920 and, on opposition turf, Vancouver in 1921. It would be another Ontario team, the Toronto St. Pats, led by Cecil "Babe" Dye, which would make headlines in 1922, taking down the Vancouver Millionaires in the final. Dye led all playoff scorers that spring with nine goals in five games.

In 1923, a major rift between Newsy Lalonde and Montreal club owner Leo Dandurand triggered a trade of the star forward to Saskatoon of the infant Western League. The compensation? Oh, only a flashy forward by the name of Aurel Joliat. At the time of the deal, Joliat was playing in Iroquois Falls and weighed a trifling 140 pounds with rocks in his pockets. But his electrifying quickness soon had Montreal fans enraptured. The infusion of excitement Joliat brought to the Canadiens wasn't enough to push them past the Ottawa Senators in the playoffs. The vicious two-game series took a physical toll on the Senators, however, and by the time they traveled west to meet the PCHA champion from Vancouver, and the Western Canada Hockey League kingpin Edmonton Eskimos, they'd been depleted by injury. But even that couldn't stall the Senators' express, prompting Frank Patrick to say they were the best team he'd ever seen.

Another national hero made his NHL debut for the Canadiens in 1923 in the form of a small (165 pounds), fearless speed merchant by the name of Howie Morenz, who was quickly nicknamed "the Stratford Streak." His like had never been seen before, on or off the ice. Morenz became one of the first, and certainly the best-known at that time, celebrity hockey stars. Morenz was the Canadian version of those larger-than-life icons in other North American professional sports, such as tennis great Bill Tilden and heavyweight champion Jack Dempsey. He was loquacious, charming; wore expensive suits and sported spats. Howie Morenz played the role of a dandy in his personal, and professional, life. Such was his swagger that Morenz was drawing comparisons to "the Sultan of Swat" himself, Yankee slugger Babe Ruth.

When Newsy Lalonde was dealt to Saskatoon of the Western League in 1923 over a contract dispute, Montreal wound up with future Hall of Famer Aurel Joliat in return.

The dazzling Aurel Joliat.

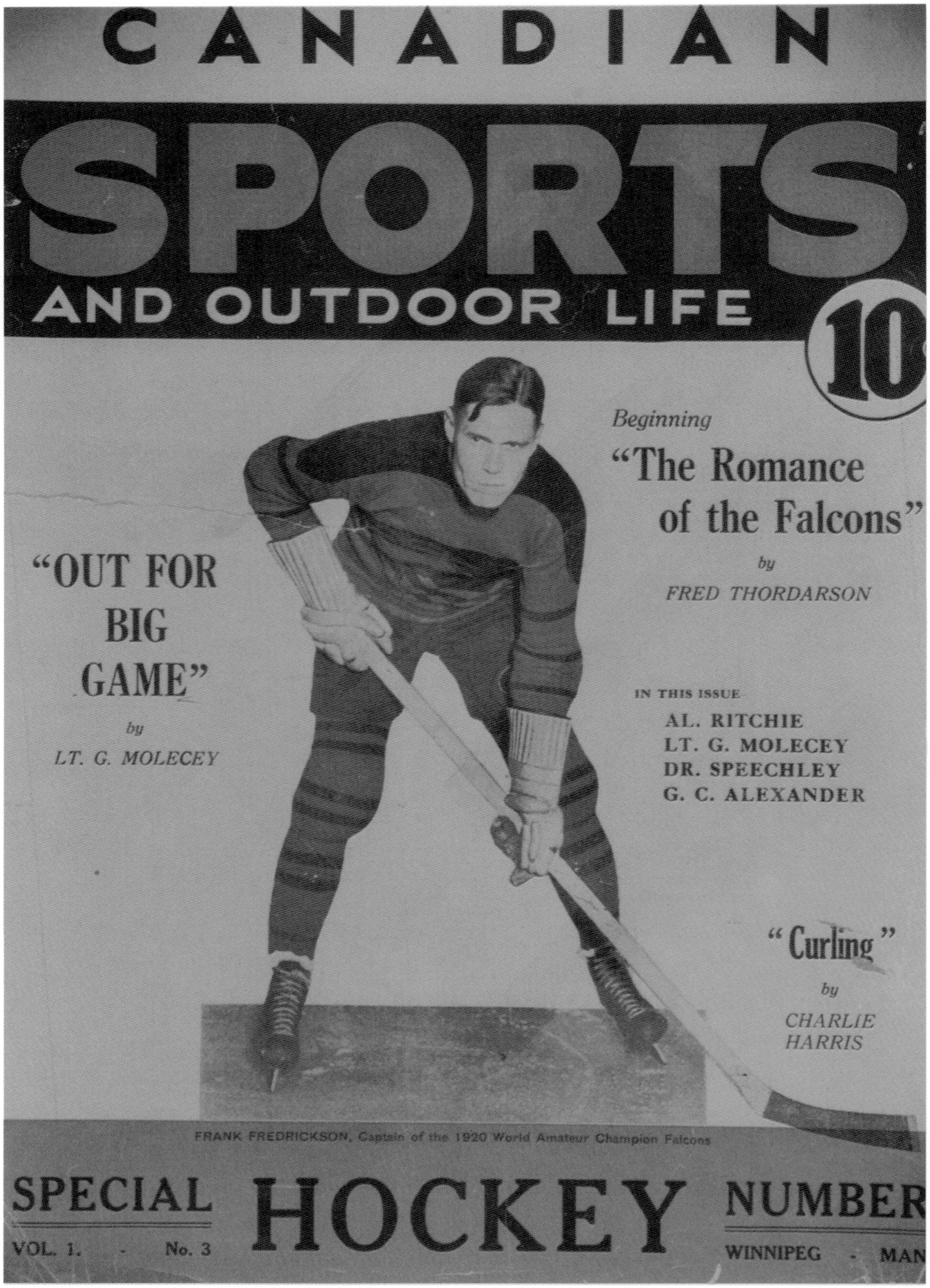

CANADIAN

SPORTS

AND OUTDOOR LIFE

10

Beginning

"The Romance of the Falcons"

by

FRED THORDARSON

"OUT FOR BIG GAME"

by

LT. G. MOLECEY

IN THIS ISSUE

AL. RITCHIE
LT. G. MOLECEY
DR. SPEECHLEY
G. C. ALEXANDER

"Curling"

by

CHARLIE HARRIS

FRANK FREDRICKSON, Captain of the 1920 World Amateur Champion Falcons

SPECIAL HOCKEY NUMBER

VOL. 1. - No. 3

WINNIPEG - MAN

A 1920 game program featuring Frank Fredrickson of the Winnipeg Falcons.

Backstopped by goalie Georges Vezina (center), the 1924 Montreal Canadiens boasted a Hall of Fame lineup, which also included Aurel Joliat and Howie Morenz.

Morenz, flanked by Joliat and Billy Boucher on his wings, would score sixty-six goals in eighty-five games between 1924 and 1926. His brilliance—complemented, of course, by Vezina in goal, Sprague Cleghorn on defense and Joliat up front—would propel the Canadiens to the 1924 championship. The Stratford Streak was injured halfway through the final game versus Calgary, when a hit sent him sprawling. He suffered torn left shoulder ligaments and a chipped collarbone. At that point, it didn't matter, as the Canadiens went on to win 3–0 and Morenz had all summer to heal.

The 1925 season witnessed the first game played in the newly completed Montreal Forum. It also saw the inclusion of Boston in the NHL. Out west, it introduced a star-to-be in one of the toughest, meanest hombres ever to grace a sheet of ice—the remarkable Eddie Shore, who skated for the Regina franchise. The 1925 finals also had its share of controversy. A strike by first-place Hamilton—which would have received a playoff elimination in the NHL following a revision of the playoff structure—over $200 the players felt was owed to them because of an increase from twenty-

Howie Morenz, the Stratford Streak, rivaled Babe Ruth and Jack Dempsey in charisma.

four to thirty games in the regular season, meant second-place Montreal and third-place Toronto eventually collided to dispute the league title.

Spearheaded by Joliat and Morenz, Montreal prevailed and went on to meet the Victoria Cougars of the Western Canada Hockey League for the Cup. After falling 5–2 in the opener, decimated by veteran left winger Jack Walker and puck-rushing defenseman Gord Fraser, who scored twice, the Canadiens made the long trek west for Game Two. Reports had a crowd standing at the corner of Peel and St. Catherine Streets in Montreal until 2 a.m. to hear telegraphic reports of the game. The news wasn't good. Led by two goals from Walker, the Cougars won 3–1, paving the way for a four-game triumph. Fraser, who must have seemed nothing so much as a deadly apparition to Montreal, scored an amazing eight goals in the series.

By 1926, a rule had been put in place that no team's payroll could exceed $35,000. The death of Georges Vezina cast a pall over the Canadiens' season. A team was awarded to Pittsburgh, to be called the Pirates, and the Hamilton franchise was sold to New York interests for $75,000. The New York team was called the Americans and they played with Madison Square Garden as their home base. Cracks were now starting to show in the status quo of the game. The Western Canada Hockey League struggled mightily and the ailing Regina franchise was shifted to Portland, causing the league to be renamed the Western Hockey League (WHL). The WHL final pitted the defending Cup champion Cougars against Edmonton, spurred by the nasty, talented, indomitable Eddie Shore, who was known by his nickname, "the Edmonton Express."

Over in the NHL, the Maroons and Ottawa

Eddie Shore, the Edmonton Express, was one of the most feared defensemen in history.

collided for the title. Montreal goaltender Clint Benedict proved he was able to play at a high level. In thirty-six regular-season games, Benedict posted a goals against average of 1.91 and six shutouts. The Maroons were counting on Benedict against Ottawa. He didn't disappoint, allowing but one goal in the two-game set. Montreal followed a bitterly fought 1–1 tie with a 1–0 victory and secured the right to face Victoria for the Cup.

The arrival of artificial ice at the Montreal Forum prevented a catastrophe in the late-starting series, which the Maroons won three games to one. It would be the last Stanley Cup contested for by teams outside of the National Hockey League umbrella. The Western Hockey League was on the verge of collapse—and indeed its talent pool would be swallowed up for $250,000, leaving the NHL as the lone survivor in an unparalleled age of change and upheaval.

The 1926–27 season would showcase a ten-team, two-division league. The first Stanley Cup era had ended, the next—the era of Howie Morenz and Lionel Conacher and Eddie Shore and Aurel Joliat and Cooney Weiland and Dit Clapper and Charlie Conacher, to name just a few—was about to begin. So much had happened since the banquet at Ottawa in May 1892, when an announcement was made that Lord Stanley had purchased a "challenge cup" and that competition for the bauble would be open to every interested challenger. The letter read at that banquet said, in part: "I have for some time been thinking it would be a good thing if there were a challenge cup which could be held from year to year by the leading hockey club in Canada. There does not appear to be any visible sign of the championship at present." Thirty-four years later, that wasn't at issue anymore. It seems ludicrous today, but when Lord Stanley originally had the Cup fashioned, it cost him ten British guineas, or roughly $50. By the mid-1920s, it was well on its way to being priceless.

Nels Stewart began his fifteen-year-long hockey career in 1925 with the Montreal Maroons. He would also play for Boston and the New York Americans.

One League, Many Legends 1927–1945

Detroit interests purchased the Victoria Tigers in 1926, called them the Cougars, renamed them the Falcons in 1930, and then the Red Wings in 1932. To bolster their early rosters, they traded for established players such as Reg Noble (above), a rugged center-defenseman acquired from the Montreal Maroons in 1927 for $7,500. Noble played six more seasons in Detroit.

Hockey's most dramatic era was framed by the ends of two wars: one financial, the other lethal. When the WCHL finally expired after the 1926 season, so, too, did the expensive bidding war between rival cross-continental pro leagues. Since Frank Calder's fraternity was now the only major professional hockey league, the trustees of the Stanley Cup decided that the NHL, and the NHL alone, should determine the terms of competition for their battered basin.

By the time World War II concluded, a few weeks after the 1945 championship, the Stanley Cup final would be all but unrecognizable to those who knew it in 1926–27. Even the nicknames of the two teams that struggled through seven games in that 1945 final, the Red Wings and Maple Leafs, did not exist in the autumn of 1926.

That year, the NHL expanded to ten teams, recruiting dozens of former WCHL players. And for the first time, American franchises outnumbered Canadian ones, six to four.

Chicago bought the entire Portland roster to form the new Black Hawks team. An eastern consortium purchased the Victoria Cougars and shifted them to Detroit, to become the Detroit Cougars, who later became the Falcons and still later, the Red Wings. Madison Square Garden, where hockey had gained immediate acceptance as a "society sport," got a second team in the Rangers. The Rangers were built with western stars recruited by Conn Smythe—"the team was born mature" according to one writer of the day—but Smythe was fired before the team played a game and replaced by the more renowned Lester Patrick. Smythe bitterly vowed that he would build another team capable of beating the Rangers, setting the tone for one of the many acrid vendettas that highlighted the era.

It was a period of Stanley Cup finals featuring bloodied, incapacitated goalies, controversial presidential decisions, physical abuse of referees and low-scoring games. In 66 percent of the

In 1924, the New York Life Insurance Company decided to raze the old Madison Square Garden for a new office tower. But boxing promoter Tex Rickard formed a syndicate to buy the property, and by December 1925, the new Garden was built with the New York Americans as tenants. A year later, the Garden bought their own expansion franchise and called them the Rangers (Tex's Rangers!).

MADISON SQ. GARDEN
WORLD'S CHAMPIONSHIP
RODEO
ROY ROGERS IN PERSON
$115 000 IN PRIZE MONEY
MATINEES FRI-SAT-SUN
AND GOLUMBUS DAY
MADISON SQ. GARDEN
DRUGS Rexall SODA

36 The original Ottawa Senators won their last Stanley Cup in 1927 in the first "world series of modern hockey" against the Boston Bruins. Cy Denneny had four of the Senators' seven goals in the finals, but he was just one of seven future Hall of Famers on a roster which had only twelve men. One of the other stars was playmaking center Frank Nighbor, whose car is shown here as part of the raucous Stanley Cup victory parade. "The Pembroke Peach" led the league in assists in 1926.

Stanley Cup final games between 1927 and 1945, neither team managed more than three goals. And there were two years, 1933 and 1934, when the Cup was won by an overtime goal that snapped a scoreless tie.

But it was also an era that created the most celebrated legends in Stanley Cup history: Lester Patrick coming off the bench to play goal at age forty-four, the original Flying Frenchmen, the Kid Line, the greatest comeback in a Cup series, Tommy Gorman, Dick Irvin and Rocket Richard's five goals.

And there was a utopian Stanley Cup equality. Although some teams, such as the Bruins, dominated the regular season for lengthy stretches, the NHL has never since enjoyed a period of such

Alex Connell, "the Ottawa Fireman," backstopped two Canadian teams to their last Stanley Cups. He allowed only four goals in six playoff games as the Ottawa Senators won the 1927 Cup. He also took the Montreal Maroons to the championship in 1935. He led the league four times in shutouts, and three times had the lowest goals against average in the playoffs.

Jack Adams played center for the Toronto St. Pats, the Vancouver Millionaires and won Stanley Cups with the 1918 Toronto Arenas and 1927 Ottawa Senators. But he is best known as the manager and coach of the Detroit Cougars/Falcons/Red Wings from 1927 to 1962. He also coached the team until 1947, winning three Stanley Cups.

championship parity as the eight springs between 1938 and 1945, when all "Original Six" teams won the Stanley Cup.

The league split into two five-team divisions for 1926–27 and kept the American and Canadian divisional format until 1938–39, when the NHL contracted to seven teams, in a single division.

For the most part, the Stanley Cup final was a best-of-five series until the NHL expanded the final to seven games in 1939. Until 1942, six teams qualified for the playoffs, with the top two meeting in the "A" or "league championship" series and the winner advancing directly to the final.

By 1942–43, the Depression and World War II had pared the NHL down to the Original Six teams and the playoff format that

When the Boston Bruins won their first Stanley Cup in 1929, over the Rangers in the first all-American final, Cecil "Tiny" Thompson became just the third NHL rookie goalie to post a shutout in the Stanley Cup final. Although he led the NHL in games played in nine of his twelve seasons, and led in wins five times for the powerful Bruins, he never won another Stanley Cup after his rookie year.

In this photo from the 1929 season, Francis "King" Clancy is wearing his Ottawa sweater and Frank Calder is sporting a bow-tie.

would stand until the grand expansion of 1967—two best-of-seven semifinals and a best-of-seven final.

But the "modern era" was really born in 1943–44, when the NHL introduced the center red line in order to reduce offside calls and speed up the game. With that major innovation—the culmination of years of tinkering with offside and forward-passing rules—the return of dozens of players from the armed forces and the retrenchment to six teams, by 1945 the NHL, and its Stanley Cup final, had finally stabilized.

The emergence of the modern game, encouraging passing and open-ice skating, represented a significant evolution over the nineteen years of the premodern era, which began with the crowded scrums of 1920s hockey.

Those scrums nourished fancy stickhandlers, accurate shooters and punishing defenders, and no team had more of them than the Ottawa Senators.

In 1926–27, the Senators had seven future Hall of Famers on their twelve-man roster: Cy Denneny, Frank Nighbor, Jack Adams

Cy Denneny was a Hall of Fame left winger for the Ottawa Senators, winning two Stanley Cups in the nation's capital, and scoring four of the Senators' seven goals in the 1927 final, including the winning goals in both of the games they won (they also tied two).

and Hooley Smith up front, King Clancy and George Boucher on defense and Alex Connell in goal. They won the Canadian Division with ease, walloped the Canadiens in the semifinals and went to Boston to open a best-of-five final in what was billed as the first "world series of modern hockey" against the colorful Bruins of Eddie Shore, Dit Clapper and goalie Tiny Thompson.

When the WCHL folded, Bruins owner Charles Adams authorized his manager, Art Ross, to spend $50,000 on seven western players. But the NHL, fearing a destructive bidding war, vetoed the deal, bought the remnants of the WCHL and held a dispersal draft. But the Bruins still got the two players they most coveted, Shore and Harry Oliver.

The opening game ended in a scoreless draw, although the Bruins had scored in the first period and Denneny scored in overtime. Both goals were called back for offside passes. NHL president Frank Calder ruled that if neither team won three games, the teams would share the Stanley Cup, but he later amended that decision. Whichever team had the most wins after four games would take the Cup.

Ottawa won the second game 3–1, and when the third game was deadlocked 1–1 after overtime, the Senators needed only a tie on home ice to clinch. The team that Canadian Press called "the poke-checkingest bunch in the history of hockey" also took the last game 3–1, with Denneny scoring the winner. He scored four of the Sens' seven goals in the final.

Boston's Billy Coutu was suspended for life for charging into referee Jerry LaFlamme during the deciding game. He was reinstated five years later, although it was too late to resume his career.

Despite the victory, there were storm clouds brewing over Ottawa. Hooley Smith had disgraced himself by butt-ending Oliver in the face during the series and was soon traded to the Montreal Maroons. Smith was never a favorite of his Senator teammates, but the deal really signaled the auctioning of stars by the cash-strapped Ottawa franchise. Smith was first, but Denneny and Clancy would soon follow.

Smith helped the Maroons beat the Senators in the opening round of the playoffs the following season. Then Russ Oatman's goal relented the next day and allowed the Rangers to use New York Americans goalie Joe Miller, who had spent most of the season with Niagara Falls in the Can-Am League. Miller lost the third game 2–0 but blanked the Maroons 1–0 in Game Four, with Boucher scoring, to tie the series.

Boucher scored both goals in the deciding game, a 2–1 victory, giving him four of the five Rangers goals in the series.

"When Conn Smythe signed the two Cooks in 1926, he asked them who they wanted to play center," Murdoch recalled. "And they said Frankie Boucher, so Conn signed him, too."

Smythe never benefited, but the team he built became the first American NHL franchise to win the Stanley Cup and made a legend out of the man who replaced him.

Just twelve months later, the Rangers met Boston in the Stanley Cup's first all-American final. In a best-of-three series, the first-place Bruins swept the exhausted Rangers on back-to-back nights for their first Stanley Cup.

Boston Garden had opened earlier that season, on November 20, 1928, and the Bruins rode home-ice advantage to a three-game sweep of the favored Canadiens in the semifinals. Little George Hainsworth, who would be prominent in several subsequent finals, had recorded a phenomenal twenty-two shutouts in forty-four league games. But he was outplayed by Boston's Cecil "Tiny" Thompson who recorded 1–0 shutouts in the first two games of the semifinals.

Meanwhile, the Rangers were surviving successive series against the Americans and Leafs, winning each in overtime of the second game.

High-scoring, and even more highly penalized, defenseman Eddie Shore was the captain and undisputed kingpin of the Bruins, and the innovative Art Ross was the manager-coach. Ross, former manager of the Hamilton Tigers, designed the nets still in use today, invented the earliest hockey helmets and became the first coach to pull his goalie in a playoff game.

Up front the Bruins were led by the "Dynamite Line" of Dit Clapper, Ralph "Cooney" Weiland and fleet Norm "Dutch" Gainor, plus Cy Denneny, purchased from the Senators just before the season.

Thompson, though, was the star of the postseason, blanking the

George Hainsworth (left) held the NHL career record for NHL shutouts with ninety-four, until it was eventually broken by Terry Sawchuk. He recorded a phenomenal twenty-two of them in a forty-four-game schedule for the 1928–29 Canadiens. But the Canadiens didn't win the Stanley Cup that season. They did win in 1930, when this picture was taken with one of his rugged defensemen, Albert "Battleship" Leduc.

Dit Clapper was the first player to last twenty seasons in the NHL, all with Boston. The Bruins won the Stanley Cup in 1941, when this photo was taken. By then he was a thirty-four-year-old defenseman. But he was a twenty-two-year-old top-scoring right winger when they won the 1929 Cup, playing on Boston's top line with Cooney Weiland and Dutch Gainor.

No wonder these 1939 Boston Bruins won the Stanley Cup. The three players shown here (Dit Clapper in the helmet, goalie Frank Brimsek and winger Woody Dumart) each were inducted into the Hockey Hall of Fame.

Rangers 2–0 in the opener and allowing only Butch Keeling's goal in a 2–1 decision at Madison Square Garden. Bruins goals were scored by Harry Oliver, Bill Carson and sophomore NHLer Clapper, who would go on to become the first player to make the First All-Star Team both as a forward and defenseman.

The Bruins, who were to finish first six times in the 1930s, had every reason to believe they were on the cusp of a dynasty. In 1929–30, they roared to their third straight division title as Weiland won the scoring title with a record seventy-three points, Clapper finished third in league scoring and Tiny Thompson went twenty-three games without a loss and established the NHL's all-time best winning percentage of .875 in losing just five of forty-four games.

Boston had seventeen more wins than the undersized Canadiens, whom they met in a best-of-three final and had beaten in all four regular-season games.

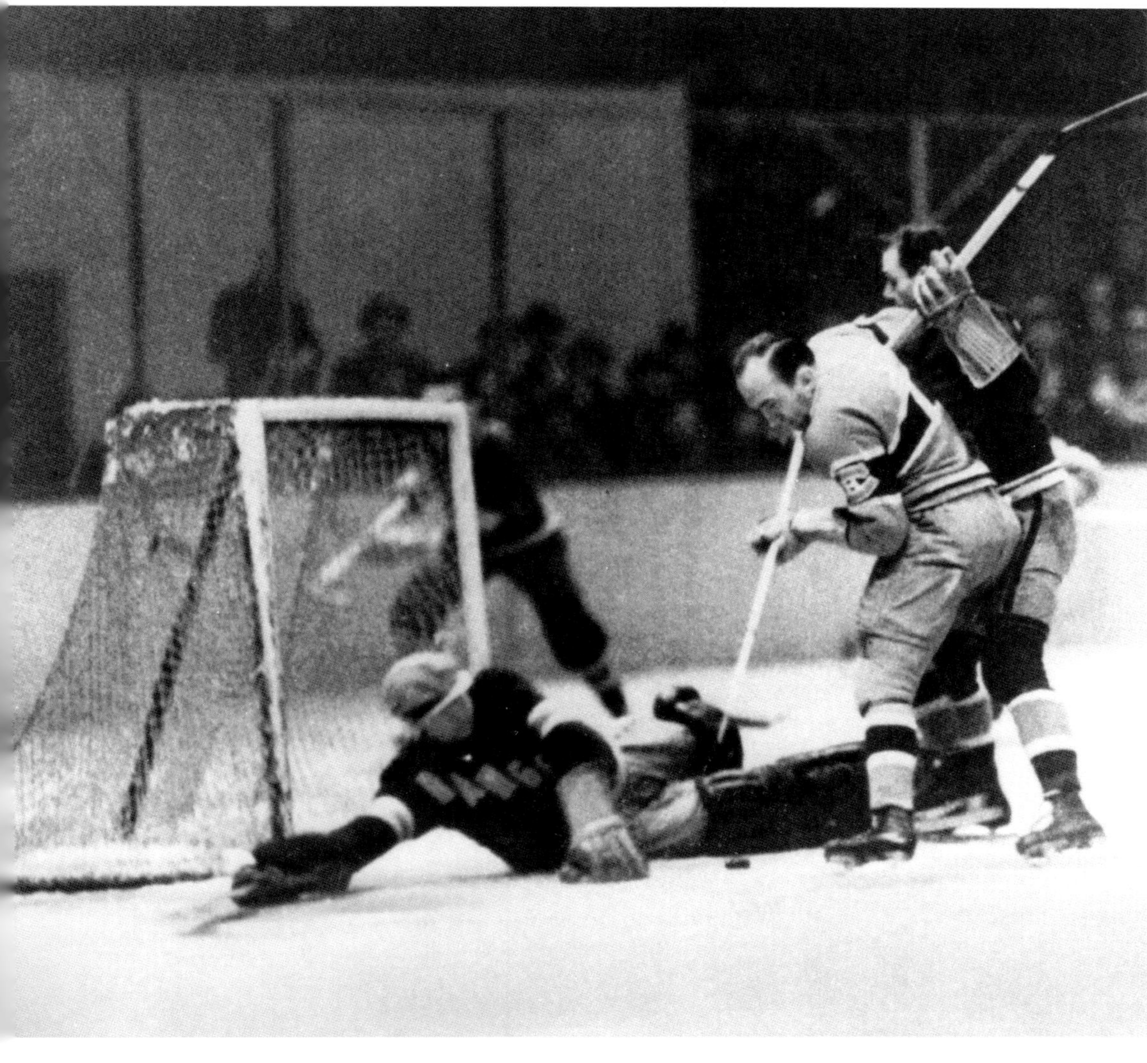

One of the most frightening sights for an NHL goalie during the 1920s and 1930s was of Howie Morenz coming in on the net. Morenz won two scoring championships and led the Canadiens in goals and assists for seven straight seasons. He helped the Canadiens become the second NHL team to repeat as Stanley Cup champions in 1930 and 1931. He was not only fast, but also played a tough game. Injuries began to affect his play and he was dealt to Chicago in 1934. He was brought back to Montreal to boost box-office sales for the 1936–37 season, but he broke his leg in a game on January 28. He died on March 8, 1937 and lay in state at the Montreal Forum. More than 10,000 mourners attended his funeral service in the Forum, one of the most famous events in the old building's history.

But by spring, the Canadiens had shifted into full "Flying Frenchmen" mode and came into the finals off two spectacular playoff series. Two nights after Howie Morenz's goal in the third overtime had eliminated the Black Hawks, Gus Rivers scored in the fourth overtime in the opener of a two-game sweep of the Rangers.

"Morenz just loped over the ice, he was such a great skater," recalled then-Ranger Murray Murdoch. "He was happy-go-lucky. He was a funny guy and didn't have anything mean about him at all. And they still had Aurel Joliat, who wore that hat while he played. He was a tricky little devil."

Canadiens manager Leo Dandurand never corrected, in fact

Aurel Joliat, shown at the New York Rangers net during a game in the 1930s, was on the fastest line of them all with Howie Morenz and the clever Johnny "Black Cat" Gagnon. Joliat was only five-foot-seven and weighed just 140 pounds. Nicknamed "the Mighty Atom" and "the Little Giant," his speed and elusiveness made him difficult to check. He was recognized as the best left winger in the league for most of his fabulous career, which stretched from 1922 to 1937.

The 1931 Canadiens had little George Hainsworth in goal, Aurel Joliat and Howie Morenz on one of the most productive lines and the Mantha brothers, Sylvio and George. They were riding the tailwind of an upset victory over Boston in the 1930 Stanley Cup finals. The Bruins got a rematch in the 1931 semifinals. Montreal lost Game Two and Game Three in lengthy overtimes but came back to win the best-of-five in three games to two.

encouraged, the mistaken belief that Morenz, the Stratford Streak, was French Canadian. It helped develop the mystique of the Flying Frenchmen.

The Bruins hadn't lost back-to-back games all season until George Hainsworth shut them out 3–0 at Boston Garden in the first game of the finals and prevailed 4–3 in Game Two back at the Forum, to give the Canadiens the Cup. Despite the fire-wagon hockey up front, it was defenseman, and captain, Sylvio Mantha who scored key goals in each game.

Morenz, Joliat and Mantha were the only holdovers from Montreal's team of 1926, and all three were back in the spring of 1931, when the Canadiens repeated as Stanley Cup champions.

Morenz won the scoring championship and the Hart trophy but did not score a goal in the Cup final against Chicago until the third period of the fifth and deciding game. That hard shot, which the goal judge said, "nearly carried the twine out of the back of the net," was the clincher in a 2–0 victory.

Both the Black Hawks and Canadiens were nearly eliminated on the way to one of the most spectacular finals ever played. Montreal won its semifinal over Boston when Morenz's linemate, Wildor Larochelle, scored in overtime in the deciding game. Chicago required an overtime goal from Stewart Adams to eliminate Toronto in the opening round.

The Black Hawks won Game Two of the finals in double overtime (on Johnny Gottselig's high shot) before 18,000 fans at Chicago Stadium, the largest crowd in hockey history, to square the Cup final. Then they won Game Three at the Forum when Cy Wentworth scored in *triple* overtime.

Chicago was within sight of its first Stanley Cup when they led 2–0 in Game Four, but Pit Lepine, another Habs speedster, scored two power play goals to tie the game. The Habs stayed alive with a

Aurel Joliat was known by his trademark hat. "He was a tricky little devil," recalls Murray Murdoch, a member of the New York Rangers for most of the years that Joliat played. The Hall of Fame left winger was owned by Saskatoon of the WCHL but never played for them. His rights were sent to Montreal, along with $3,500, in September 1922 for Newsy Lalonde, who was then thirty-four years old. It was one of the best trades the Canadiens ever made.

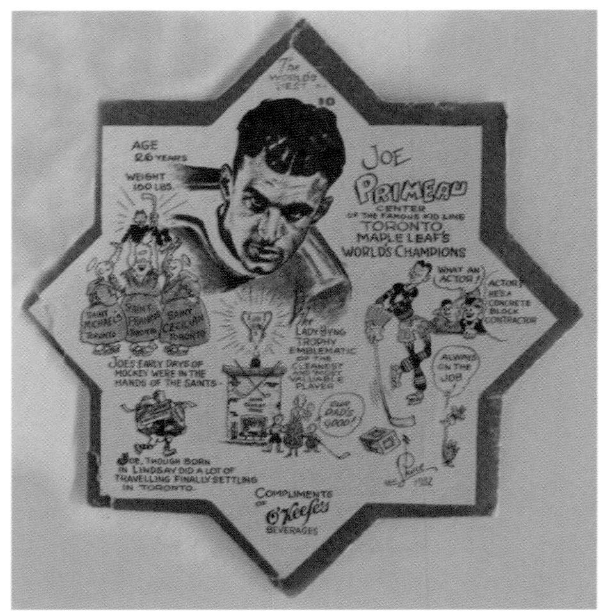

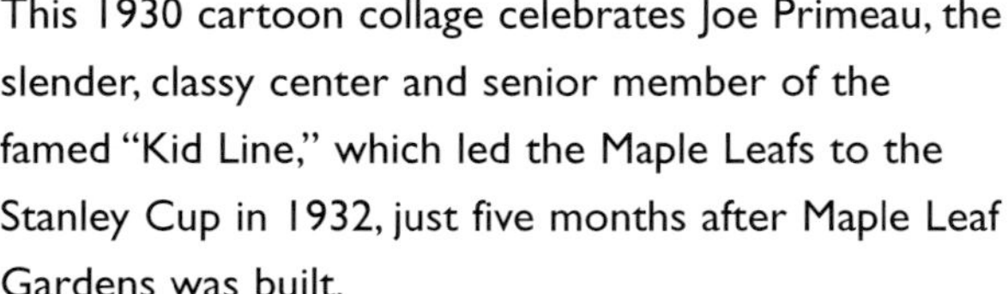
This 1930 cartoon collage celebrates Joe Primeau, the slender, classy center and senior member of the famed "Kid Line," which led the Maple Leafs to the Stanley Cup in 1932, just five months after Maple Leaf Gardens was built.

When Conn Smythe was fired by the New York Rangers in 1926 before the team he'd assembled had even played a game, he vowed he would someday build a team capable of beating the Broadway Blueshirts. In 1927 he purchased the Toronto St. Pats, changed their name to the Maple Leafs and their colors from green and white to blue and white and eventually won the Stanley Cup with the team pictured here in 1932.

Although Dick Irvin was the coach, owner and general manager, Conn Smythe often gave pep talks to his Maple Leaf teams, as he's seen doing here. Although they had some of the most famous players in the game—the Kid Line, King Clancy, Red Horner, Frank Finnigan—Smythe's Leafs won only one Stanley Cup in the first fourteen years of the franchise.

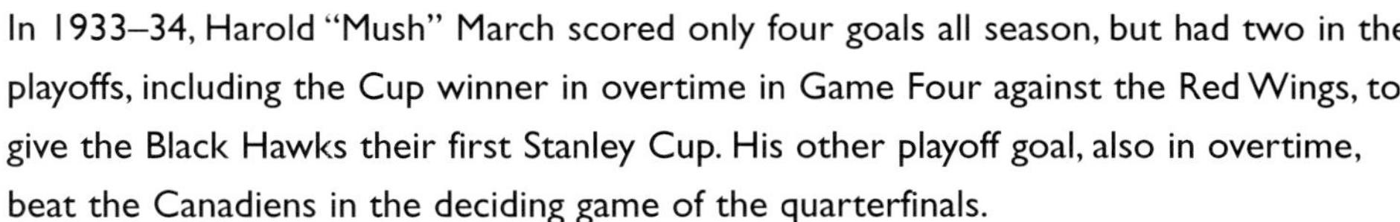

In 1933–34, Harold "Mush" March scored only four goals all season, but had two in the playoffs, including the Cup winner in overtime in Game Four against the Red Wings, to give the Black Hawks their first Stanley Cup. His other playoff goal, also in overtime, beat the Canadiens in the deciding game of the quarterfinals.

Toronto Maple Leafs' Ace Bailey led the NHL in goals and total points in 1928–29. He later transformed himself into a defensive specialist and helped the Leafs to their first Cup win in 1932.

4–2 victory, but their fans, thinking the Hawks had played too roughly, pelted the officials with coins, programs and a bottle of gin, which missed referee Bobby Hewitson by only a couple of inches.

The audience was much happier three nights later when Johnny Gagnon took a clever drop pass from Joliat in the second period of the deciding game and scored the go-ahead goal. Morenz clinched it in the next period, but at the end of the game, it was Black Hawk goalie Chuck Gardiner whom the Canadiens hoisted on their shoulders. Gardiner had been sensational throughout the series.

American sportswriting legend Grantland Rice wrote of the Canadiens, "It is only proper that a world's championship hockey pennant should be flown under Canadian skies. Canada is largely responsible for a game that is getting bigger, better, faster and more

Harvey "Busher" Jackson was the left winger and youngest member of the Maple Leafs' famous Kid Line with Charlie Conacher and Joe Primeau. He led the NHL scoring in 1932.

The Chicago Black Hawks won their first Stanley Cup in 1934. They won the series against Detroit three games to one. In their three wins, goalie Chuck Gardiner allowed only two goals. Gardiner had been gravely ill all season and died of a brain hemorrhage eight weeks after hoisting the Cup.

popular every year. Canada supplies in speed and spirit what it lacks in competitive numbers."

The Cup, or "pennant," as Rice would have it, remained in Canada in 1932 when the Toronto Maple Leafs finally made good on Conn Smythe's six-year-old promise to build a team that would beat the Rangers.

Smythe's Leafs rode the "Kid Line" to a three-game sweep over the Rangers, the uncharacteristic scores reading like a tennis match: 6–4, 6–2, 6–4.

Gentleman Joe Primeau, the elder statesman of the Kid Line at

In the first all-Canadian final in nine years, the Maroons easily handled the Maple Leafs in three straight games with the great Alex Connell permitting only four goals. Three years after winning their second Stanley Cup in 1935, the Montreal Maroons succumbed to the declining hockey economy in Montreal and folded, leaving the market to the Canadiens.

age twenty-six, led the NHL in assists. Big right winger Charlie Conacher, twenty-two, was the best of a famous hockey-playing family and would lead the NHL in goals five times, including 1931–32 when he tied Bill Cook with thirty-four. The left winger was the magnetic Harvey "Busher" Jackson, twenty-one. All three members of the Kid Line had played for Frank Selke's Toronto Marlboros, as had fellow Leafs Alex Levinsky, the battle-scarred Red Horner and Bob Gracie, who put the Leafs into the 1932 Cup final with an overtime goal against the Montreal Maroons.

Maple Leaf Gardens had opened in November of that season, but

Cy Wentworth was the defensive mainstay for the Chicago Black Hawks, Montreal Maroons and Montreal Canadiens in his thirteen-year career. In 1935, he had just thirteen points in the forty-eight-game regular season, but in the low-scoring playoffs, he led all scorers with five points, including three important goals.

Toronto slid into last place after a dozen games. Smythe, trying to equal his marquee acquisition of King Clancy the previous autumn, attempted to buy Howie Morenz from the Canadiens and then Johnny Gottselig from the Black Hawks. Rebuffed on both fronts, Smythe instead fired coach Art Duncan and brought in the hockey innovator from Saskatchewan, Dick Irvin, who had led the Black Hawks into the finals the year before.

Each game of the finals was played in a different "Garden." The Leafs won the opener in Madison Square Garden in what nationally renowned radio play-by-play broadcaster Foster Hewitt called "the ultimate hockey game." The Kid Line scored four times, with Jackson getting three goals and an assist, while the 150-pound Clancy was robust on the blue line. The annual arrival of the circus forced Game Two to the Boston Garden (which was felt to be a neutral site), where the Kid Line led the Leafs back from a 2–0 deficit to a 6–2 win. Conacher and Clancy scored twice, Jackson once and Primeau had three assists.

Jackson scored twice in the clinching 6–4 victory at Maple Leaf Gardens, and Toronto had its first Stanley Cup since the St. Pats won it ten years earlier. The Kid Line had beaten the fabulous Cook Brothers–Boucher line Smythe had recruited for New York. And Lorne Chabot, whom he'd obtained for the Rangers, was now his goalie in Toronto.

The Rangers didn't have to wait long to avenge the loss, as they dismissed the Leafs three games to one in the 1933 final.

Toronto had eliminated Boston in the deciding match of the semifinal when Ken Doraty scored after 164 minutes and forty-six seconds of overtime, the second-longest NHL game ever played. The exhausted Leafs were no match for the rested, and motivated, Rangers, who won 5–1 the next night at Madison Square Garden. Again, the circus invaded New York and the last three games were all at Maple Leaf Gardens.

"That was fine with us," said Murdoch. "It made it easy. We were together as a team and teamwork meant a lot in those days."

Bill Cook's goal broke a scoreless tie at 7:33 of overtime in Game Four, the first time a Stanley Cup had ever been decided in extra time.

An overtime goal also ended the next season. Harold "Mush"

These 1937 Detroit Red Wings were the first American team to repeat as Stanley Cup champions. They had only a dozen healthy players when the final against the Rangers opened and they lost Vezina Trophy–winner Norm Smith in the first game. With Smith playing well earlier in the season, the Red Wings were ready to sell one of their two minor league goalies, and the Toronto Maple Leafs chose Turk Broda instead of Earl Robertson. When Smith was hurt, Robertson played the rest of the games against the Rangers and became the first rookie to earn two shutouts in the finals.

March's power play shot broke a scoreless tie halfway through the second extra period, giving the Black Hawks their first championship, in four games over Detroit.

The defensive-minded Hawks also won the opening game in double overtime, with Paul Thompson scoring from close range over Detroit goalie Wilf Cude's shoulder. Chuck Gardiner, who, like Cude, learned his goaltending skills in Winnipeg, permitted only two goals in the three Chicago wins, covering 231 minutes and fifteen seconds of play. Eight weeks after the series, he died of a brain hemorrhage.

The Hawks were managed by the colorful Tommy Gorman, a P. T. Barnum type who'd been a racetrack owner, sports editor of the *Ottawa Citizen* and the former owner of the Ottawa Senators. Canadiens executives Leo Dandurand and Joe Cattarinch, who had $50,000 in the Black Hawks and wanted someone to keep an eye on their investment, persuaded Chicago owner Major Frederic McLaughlin to accept Gorman.

But with the Wirtzes taking over in Chicago, Gorman knew he'd be fired. So right after his team won the Cup, he packed his belongings in his car and drove back to Canada, where he immediately found a job with the struggling Montreal Maroons.

Gorman led those Maroons to their last great hurrah, with a three-game sweep of heavily favored Toronto in the 1935 Stanley Cup final. It was the first all-Canadian final since 1926 and the last

Herbie Lewis celebrates the Red Wings' 1936 Stanley Cup victory. The Wings finally won the franchise's first Cup on April 11, 1936, beating the Maple Leafs in the fourth game of a best-of-five final. Lewis was the left winger on Detroit's top line, with center Marty Barry (obtained that year in a trade with Boston) and right winger Larry Aurie. Barry was second in league scoring in 1936, while Lewis was ninth with thirty-seven points, just eight back of leader Sweeney Schriner of the New York Americans.

one for the Maroons, who would expire with barely a whimper three years later.

The series matched two aging netminders in thirty-seven-year-old George Hainsworth, the Leaf often described as "the world's most nonchalant goalie," and Alex Connell, thirty-three, who was playing against King Clancy, Frankie Finnigan and Hec Kilrea, his teammates with the champion 1927 Senators.

Connell was spectacular, particularly in the Maroons' 3–1 victory in Game Two, when he stopped twenty-one shots in the first period alone. The Kid Line scored only one goal in the three-game series, as Baldy Northcott, Jimmy Ward and Hooley Smith smothered them.

Earl Robertson played all his 190 regular-season games with the New York/Brooklyn Americans but it was with the Detroit Red Wings that he made his mark. When starting goalie Norm Smith was hurt in Game One of the 1937 Stanley Cup finals, minor-leaguer Robertson stepped in and blanked the Rangers in the final two games, becoming the first rookie goalie to record two Stanley Cup shutouts. But the unsentimental Jack Adams traded him to the Americans soon after, and he recorded a shutout in his first game with them.

The forechecking Montrealers had more depth and outscored Toronto 10–4 over the three games.

The Leafs lost the final again in 1936, dropping three of four games to the Red Wings, who won the first Stanley Cup of their ten-year existence. En route, Detroit won three straight over the Maroons, including the longest game ever played, decided on Mud Bruneteau's goal after 116 minutes and thirty seconds of overtime.

The powerful Wings, coached by Jack Adams, outscored the Leafs 18–11, including a 9–4 win in Game Two, the highest winning score in a Cup final game since 1917.

Detroit clinched the championship with a 3–2 win in Toronto. The Kid Line was reunited for that game, because it was Joe Primeau's last in the NHL. Fittingly, Primeau scored the opening

Paul Goodman was caught up in the many controversial presidential rulings that were the trademark of NHL playoffs in the 1930s. Regular Chicago netminder Mike Karakas had a broken toe and could not play in the first game of the finals against the Maple Leafs. Minor leaguer Alfie Moore, owned b the New York Americans, played Game Two, but NHL president Frank Calder ruled him ineligible. So the Black Hawks turned to the thirty-three-year-ol Goodman, who had spent the last three years in Wichita with the American Hockey Association and had never played an NHL game. The Leafs beat him 5–1 for their only victory in the series, as Karakas returned for the fourth and final game. Goodman returned to the minors but did play part of two la seasons with the Hawks.

The 1938–39 Bruins were described by writers of the day as the "greatest team of all time." The Bruins ran away with the regular season amassing seventy-four points—sixteen better than the runner-up Rangers. It was the first season of the best-of-seven finals and the Bruins, with a much deeper lineup, had no trouble in taking the Maple Leafs in five games. Their only difficulty was with the Rangers in the best-of-seven semifinal, which they won 4–3, with three of their victories in overtime, including a triple overtime in the deciding game. Mel Hill, a then-obscure right winger, earned his "Sudden Death" nickname and a place in history by scoring all three overtime goals for the Bruins, two of them in triple overtime.

Before he had played his fourth NHL game, Frank Brimsek had earned the nickname that would stick with him forever. "Mr. Zero" recorded shutouts in his first three NHL games, won eight of his first ten starts, won the Calder Cup as top rookie, the Vezina Trophy as top goalie and led the Bruins to the Stanley Cup.

goal. It was also King Clancy's last playoff game on the blue line. He retired early the next season but later became a referee and worked twenty Stanley Cup finals.

The 1937 playoffs opened under the cloud of Howie Morenz's death, just two weeks earlier. His Canadiens, though, nearly beat defending champion Detroit in the semifinals, losing the deciding game on Hec Kilrea's goal in the third overtime period.

The finals were equally as riveting, as the Rangers, who had the fewest points of the six playoff teams, took Detroit to the five-game limit.

The Red Wings had only a dozen healthy skaters and were without the NHL's leading goal scorer, Larry Aurie. The Red Wings also lost Vezina Trophy winner Norman Smith in Game One when he reaggravated an earlier elbow injury. He was replaced by rookie Earl Robertson, who would never play a regular-season game for the Red Wings.

After the Rangers took a 2–1 lead in the series, Robertson was unbeatable. He shut out the Rangers 1–0 in Game Four to set up the rubber match. Marty Barry, the Wings' leading point getter, scored a goal in the first period, one in the third and assisted on another in the second period as Detroit prevailed 3–0. The turning point came with the Wings up 1–0 in the second period when Robertson easily stopped Alex Shibicky on a penalty shot.

Detroit manager-coach Jack Adams was so excited with the win that he fainted after the game and had to be revived with smelling salts.

Robertson was the first rookie to record two shutouts in the Stanley Cup finals, but three weeks later Adams traded him. Robertson earned a shutout in his first start for the New York Americans the next season.

The Red Wings, perhaps looking ahead to a Cup repeat, collapsed near the end of the 1937–38 schedule, allowing Chicago to overtake them by two points for the final playoff spot.

The Black Hawks surprised both the Canadiens and Americans to reach the final against the Leafs, who boasted NHL scoring champion Gordie Drillon and sophomore goalie sensation Turk Broda. Chicago, meanwhile, was without regular netminder Mike Karakas who had broken a toe against the New York Americans.

Rookie Alf Pike, nicknamed "the Embalmer," set the tone for the 1940 Stanley Cup finals by beating Turk Broda for a 2–1 Rangers victory in overtime in Game One.

Hawks coach Bill Stewart wanted to use the Rangers' Dave Kerr, but Conn Smythe refused. He did agree, however, to Alfie Moore of the Americans. Stewart and Smythe reportedly came to blows over the issue before Game One, but Stewart had the last laugh when Moore beat the Leafs 3–1.

League president Frank Calder ruled Moore ineligible for Game Two, and Chicago was forced to call up Paul Goodman from Wichita of the American Hockey Association. The Leafs feasted on him 5–1.

But Karakas was back for Game Three, wearing a special steel-toed skate, and he beat the Leafs 2–1 on Doc Romnes' disputed goal with four minutes to play. The Leafs claimed the shot did not enter the net, but referees Babe Dye and Clarence Campbell agreed with the goal judge, who said it did. It was sweet revenge for Romnes, who was wearing a football helmet to protect his nose that had been broken, he said, by Red Horner. The goal was witnessed by a Chicago Stadium crowd of 18,497, the largest ever for an NHL game.

The audience was slightly smaller two nights later as the Hawks

Bryan Hextall was a sturdy right winger from Saskatchewan who won the 1941–42 scoring title and made it into the Hall of Fame with 187 career goals for the New York Rangers. But none were more important than his goal at 2:07 of overtime on April 13, 1940. It gave the Rangers the Stanley Cup in six games over Toronto, and was the last New York Cup win for fifty-four years.

They could never have this nickname today, but Boston's Kraut Line was the most famous trio in an era of legendary lines. (Left to right) Bobby Bauer, Milt Schmidt and Woody Dumart dominated the NHL in 1939–40, becoming the first line to finish one-two-three in NHL scoring. The line led the Bruins to the 1941 Stanley Cup, but the entire line went into the service during the next season and finished the year winning the Allan Cup for the Ottawa RCAF.

clinched their second Cup 4–1, using eight Americans, the most ever on a championship team.

That was the last of the best-of-five finals, as the NHL expanded the championship round to a best-of-seven affair in 1939. The "A" series between division winners also went to seven games, with Boston rookie Mel Hill earning his immortal "Sudden Death Hill" sobriquet with three overtime goals against the Rangers, including the series clincher in forty-eight minutes of extra time. Hill also scored twice in the finals against Toronto, while teammate Frank "Mr. Zero" Brimsek limited the Maple Leafs to six goals in five games.

Leaf coach Dick Irvin, who lost his sixth final of the 1930s, tried to shake his team up in the final game by benching a couple of veterans in favor of minor-league call-ups, but that was a tactic that would only work for Irvin's successor, Hap Day, three springs later.

Eddie Shore was a stalwart on the Bruins' defense, and the Stanley Cup presentation ceremony was interrupted by 17,000

Boston Garden fans chanting, "We want Shore, we want Shore!" The crusty, future Hall of Famer had just played his last Stanley Cup final.

The New York Rangers beat the Shore-less Bruins in the 1940 semifinals, then took the Toronto Maple Leafs in six games to win the Stanley Cup.

It was an unusual final, not so much because the last four games were played in Toronto—the circus was at Madison Square Garden again—but because one of the cities was in a country that had declared war, and the other in a country that had not.

"When we came up to Toronto, you noticed all the uniforms and the rationing; you certainly didn't see that in New York," recalled Clint Smith, the Rangers center who set up a key goal in the pivotal fifth game.

"When you scored in Toronto, you could hear a match drop. You didn't have a single person in the building for you. Foster Hewitt was on the air and we knew the games were going west. Those New York teams were mostly western guys and Foster was very Toronto-biased. So we loved to beat Toronto."

With Vezina Trophy winner Dave Kerr in goal, a sturdy defense and scoring touch up front with Bryan Hextall, Muzz and Lynn Patrick (Lester's sons) and the Colville brothers, Mac and Neil, beat them they did. Three of the four games the Rangers won were decided in overtime, including the last two, 2–1 and 3–2 thrillers. Muzz Patrick scored the winning goal in the last game on a breakaway after the Leafs pressed heavily and buzzed the Rangers' net, a tactic that was rarely used in Stanley Cup overtime.

"If Toronto had won, Smythe and Irvin would have been hailed as heroes and masterminds," Lester Patrick said. "To me their strategy will always seem smart, no matter who takes the series."

Bill "Cowboy" Cowley stickhandled his way into the Hall of Fame after a dozen brilliant seasons with the powerful Boston Bruins in the late 1930s and 1940s. He was the league's MVP in 1941, when the Bruins won their last Cup for twenty-nine years, and he was MVP again in 1943.

Clarence Day was so outgoing that he was never known by his given name, but by the moniker "Happy." He was the Leafs' first captain and key player in their 1932 Stanley Cup win. In 1940 he became coach of the Leafs and won five Stanley Cups over the next decade.

Charlie Conacher, Joe Primeau and Busher Jackson had all played for Frank Selke's Toronto Marlboroughs, and in 1930 the trio were united as the Kid Line, the most famous trio in the Maple Leafs' history. They were the offensive punch for the Leafs' first Stanley Cup win in 1932, the season Maple Leaf Gardens opened. Conacher won four scoring titles and led the league in goals five times.

His Rangers took the series when Hextall made a brilliant rush to score in overtime.

"The Rangers finished the season with the same fifteen men who started it," said an uncharacteristically gracious Smythe. "I think that's one of the greatest accomplishments in modern hockey history."

The Rangers could never have suspected that it would be the last time for fifty-four years that a New York team would hoist the Cup.

"We sure as hell didn't," Clint Smith said, some sixty years later.

Another team that was about to embark on a long Cup-less voyage took the championship in 1941. The Boston Bruins were the class of the league, with crafty center Bill Cowley averaging nearly an assist per game to run away with the scoring title. His teammates, the "Kraut Line" of Milt Schmidt, Woody Dumart and Bobby Bauer, had finished one-two-three in scoring the previous season.

Boston endured a tough semifinal against the Leafs before Mel Hill got the winner in the seventh game, although for once it wasn't

Jack Adams, shown here celebrating the 1943 Stanley Cup win with two of his Detroit Red Wings, had a solid career as a player, but it was as a coach and general manager upon which his Hall of Fame reputation was founded. When the Wings won the fifth and deciding game of the 1937 Cup final, the fiery Adams fainted. In 1942, his Wings became the first team to blow a 3–0 lead in games, losing the Cup final to the Maple Leafs. Adams was suspended from the series after accosting the referee, and he always claimed that Conn Smythe and the Toronto media controlled that series. Adams's Wings won twelve regular-season championships, and seven Stanley Cups.

Syd Howe, shown here in 1938, won three Stanley Cups with the Detroit Red Wings (in 1936, 1937 and 1942). He was purchased from the financially distressed St. Louis Eagles for the then-astronomical sum of $50,000 in 1935. His arrival solidified the Red Wings as a perennial contender.

in overtime. Detroit did need an overtime goal from Gus Giesebrecht to eliminate the Black Hawks.

Every game in the final was close, but the Bruins were too powerful for the Wings and became the first team to sweep a Stanley Cup final in four games. They would not win again until Bobby Orr's famous flying overtime shot nearly thirty years later.

Only 8,125 fans showed up at the Olympia for Game Four, thinking that a three-game deficit was impossible to surmount. It was that April, but certainly not the next.

The Red Wings were surprise qualifiers for the 1942 Stanley Cup final, having finished fifth, fifteen points back of the second-place Leafs. But after three games, which they'd won by increasing margins—3–2, 4–2 and 5–2—Detroit stood just sixty minutes from a hockey monopoly. The Wings' farm teams in Indianapolis and Omaha had won their respective championships and now the parent club was about to win the Stanley Cup.

"They're unbeatable," said Toronto goalie Turk Broda. "They can't do anything wrong."

But in one of the most famous moves in Stanley Cup history, Leaf coach Hap Day made a dramatic change in his lineup for Game Four at the Olympia. He removed leading scorer Gordie Drillon, veteran defenseman Bucko McDonald and left winger Hank Goldup in favor of Gaye Stewart, Ernie Dickens, fringe forward Don Metz and nineteen-year-old rookie defenseman Bob Goldham.

Detroit led Game Four 2–0 in the second period and were up 3–2 with just fourteen minutes left, before captain Syl Apps and Nick Metz, Don's brother, scored for the Leafs to stave off elimination. Detroit coach Jack Adams was suspended indefinitely for throwing punches at referee Mel Harwood after the game—a charge he vehemently denied.

Don Metz had joined his brother on Apps' line and scored three goals to pace Toronto's 9–3 victory in Game Five at Maple Leaf Gardens. Notably, ex-Leaf King Clancy was the referee.

The Leafs knotted the series two nights later in Detroit as the rejuvenated Broda blanked the suddenly featherless Wings 3–0. Metz opened the scoring by stealing the puck from Sid Abel, and Goldham and Billy Taylor put the game away with third-period scores.

That set the stage for the seventh game before a Canadian-record 16,218 fans at Maple Leaf Gardens. Detroit's Syd Howe scored the only goal over a scrambly two periods, but the Leafs rallied in the third.

Sweeney Schriner, playing on his first Cup winner in eight NHL seasons, scored two goals, but the winner came on a fluke goal by Pete Langelle. A rebound flew high over Wings goalie Johnny Mowers's shoulder and landed behind him, right on Langelle's stick.

It was the first, and last, time a team was able to rebound from a 3–0 deficit in games to win the Stanley Cup, and as the trophy was

and the ubiquitous Tommy Gorman as manager, Montreal finished twenty-five points ahead of second-place Detroit. After losing the first game of the semifinals to the Leafs, the Habs won eight straight to capture their first Stanley Cup in thirteen years.

The legend of Maurice "the Rocket" Richard was born in the first of those eight wins, on March 23, 1944. Richard, playing on the famed "Punch Line" with Elmer Lach and Toe Blake, scored all five goals in the Canadiens' 5–1 victory. He would also record the first of his record three Stanley Cup finals hat tricks in Game Two of the Canadiens' sweep of the Black Hawks.

"He was a guy who, when he had the puck twenty-five to thirty feet from the net, just aimed for the net, he went to the net with everything," recalled 1944 teammate Bob Fillion. "The big chance he got was when Dick Irvin decided to use him on the right wing, even though he was a left-handed shot. Lach would slow down a bit just at the blue line. Maurice would try to skate behind the defenseman and Lach used a flip pass to get it to him.

"I remember the day when he got the five goals, he had to move furniture into his house. It was on the second floor, so he had to climb those steep stairways. He mentioned to Dick Irvin before the game that he wasn't sure he could even play. Then he scored five."

The Punch Line scored ten of the Canadiens' sixteen goals in the finals, and Blake established a new playoff record with eighteen points. He got five of them in the Habs' 5–4 victory in the last game, setting up the first four goals, then scoring the Cup winner at 9:12 of overtime.

In 1944–45, the Canadiens dominated the regular season, with Lach, Richard and Blake duplicating the Kraut Line's feat by finishing one-two-three in scoring. Richard became the first player to score fifty goals and notched a hat trick in Game Five of the semifinals, but the Leafs eliminated the Canadiens in six games.

For the first time, two rookie goalies met in a Stanley Cup final. Eighteen-year-old Harry Lumley was in net for the Detroit Red Wings and the Leafs had twenty-six-year-old Frank "Ulcers" McCool replacing Turk Broda, who was doing army service.

McCool, whose surname belied his jumpy demeanor, had been discharged from the army with stomach ulcers but played well enough to win the Calder Cup as the NHL's top rookie. And he

Babe Pratt (left) and Frank McCool (right) of the 1944–45 Toronto Maple Leafs chat with a couple of minor hockey players. The Leafs won the Stanley Cup that season with stout defensive play against the two most prolific scoring teams of the era, Montreal and Detroit. Pratt was a six-foot-three, 212-pound defenseman who'd won a Cup with the 1940 Rangers. In 1946 he was suspended for wagering on games but was reinstated fifteen days later. McCool was a twenty-six-year-old rookie from Calgary who had been discharged from the army due to ulcers. He replaced Leaf goalie Turk Broda who, ironically, was in the service. McCool shut out the Red Wings in the first three games of the final, an NHL record. After the Wings tied the series with three wins, McCool held Detroit to one goal right in the Detroit Olympia, as the Leafs prevailed 2–1 in the seventh and final game. After playing all fifty of Toronto's games that rookie season, he played only twenty-two the next year, and retired from the game.

Harry Lumley made his Stanley Cup debut with the 1944–45 Detroit Red Wings as an eighteen-year-old rookie. Nicknamed "Apple Cheeks," Lumley shut out the Leafs in Games Five and Six of the Cup final, as the Red Wings rallied after Toronto had won the first three games—all on Frank McCool shutouts. The Leafs beat Lumley 2–1 in Game Seven, but the Detroit crowd chanted Lumley's name after the game was over. He led all playoff goalies in goals against average that year, a feat he never repeated in a Hall of Fame career. He did lead the league in shutouts three times, won the 1954 Vezina Trophy and played goal for every Original Six team except the Canadiens.

didn't allow the Wings, who'd gone 8–1–1 against Toronto that season, a goal until the fourth game of the Cup final. His three consecutive shutouts were a Stanley Cup record, and Toronto sat on the edge of a four-game sweep.

After Game Three, Wings veteran Mud Bruneteau sighed, "They can't be that good, we'll have to win four straight."

They almost did. Despite a hat trick by nineteen-year-old Leaf center Teeder Kennedy, Detroit won Game Four. In a bizarre near-reversal of the famous 1942 Cup final, the Wings also won the next two, both on Lumley shutouts, to force a seventh game at the Olympia.

The Leafs prevailed 2–1 to capture their third Stanley Cup, but after the game, the Detroit crowd screamed, "We want Lumley!" and the dejected goalie was brought back to the ice from the dressing room. Lumley would go on to a Hall of Fame career and McCool would play only twenty-two more NHL games.

The upright Frank Selke had been essentially running the Maple Leafs while Major Conn Smythe was commanding his own regiment in Europe. There had never been much more than a cool respect between the two men, and Selke had offended the self-important Smythe by not consulting him when he obtained Kennedy's rights from Montreal.

Despite building the framework of a Stanley Cup dynasty, Selke's days in Toronto were numbered. When World War II ended, there would not be room in Maple Leaf Gardens for both hockey giants.

The Last Cup Battles of the Original Six 1946–1967

Maple Leaf managing director Conn Smythe got so mad at Toronto's 1946 losing team that he reshaped it into the squad that won the next three Stanley Cups.

Frank Selke, Smythe's long-time assistant, was bounced from his job in 1946, but landed on his feet in Montreal with many Cup winners.

In the spring of 1946, Conn Smythe was mad at practically everybody. This hardly seemed surprising, given Smythe's habitually irascible nature, but the explosion of 1946 was singular in its range and depth. Smythe was sore at Ed Bickle, the most influential member of the Maple Leaf Gardens board of directors, because he suspected that Bickle was angling to dump him from his job as the Maple Leaf hockey club's managing director. He was furious with his own assistant, Frank Selke, believing that Selke, a Bickle man, had his eye on Smythe's office. And he was angry at the Leaf players because, after winning the Stanley Cup in 1944–45, they drooped to fifth place in the 1945–46 regular-season standings, out of the playoffs, thus paving the way for the Montreal Canadiens to beat the Boston Bruins for that year's Cup.

In order to relieve his various temper tantrums, Smythe embarked on corrective measures. He bought 30,000 Gardens shares from another director, Percy Gardiner, enough to persuade the board to name Smythe to the presidency of the whole place. That took care of Bickle and put Smythe in the driver's seat for the shaping of future Stanley Cup teams. As for Selke, Smythe goaded him by leaving a memo on his Gardens desk, instructing him never to leave the building without Smythe's prior permission.

"Lincoln freed the slaves in 1865," Selke wrote in an answering memo. "I'm gone. Goodbye."

Smythe let Selke go. He let a large complement of his players go, too, mostly elderly parties whose careers were flagging. For 1946–47, Smythe was streamlining with rookies, six of them, a radically high number in those days. To give the new crew a dash of experienced balance, Smythe retained such reliable veterans as goalie Turk Broda, incomparable under pressure, and the ever graceful center and team captain, Syl Apps. Ted Kennedy, coming off a poor season made worse by a debilitating tendon injury, was nevertheless expected to add depth, and so was a young guy who had played only thirty-two NHL games but was destined to become

Maple Leaf Gardens was home to eight Toronto Cup champs from 1946 to 1967 but to no others for the rest of the twentieth century.

78 The Leafs of 1949 dithered to a fourth-place finish in the regular season, then perked up at playoff time to bounce Detroit in four straight in the Cup finals.

C
A

ABOVE: In 1946, the first post-war NHL season, it was the veteran Canadiens, coached by Dick Irvin (front row, far left), who breezed to the Stanley Cup.

Jimmy Peters, a smart, tough forward with four teams incluc the Canadiens, won no less than four Stanley Cups in his nir NHL seasons.

These three played as a unit for most of the 1940s—Maurice Richard, Elmer Lach and Toe Blake—and in one season, 1945, they finished one-two-three in scoring, a feat that helped to earn their nickname: the "Punch Line."

Strength down the middle was what the Leafs had with three magnificent centers in the 1948 Stanley Cup winners: Ted Kennedy, Max Bentley and Syl Apps.

hockey's ace bodychecker, the indestructible "Wild Bill" Ezinicki.

This mixed bunch turned out to be an offensive powerhouse, scoring 209 goals in the season, far more than any other team. Toward the end of the year, the young defense also tightened up enough to get the Leafs into the Stanley Cup finals against the Canadiens, who had finished on top in the regular season. Montreal bombed Toronto in the first game 6–0, and Canadiens goalie Bill Durnan, scorning the Leafs, said to Elmer Ferguson of the *Montreal*

Toronto's Turk Broda was the goalie with the real reason for smiles: his Leafs had just won the 1947 Cup over Bill Durnan's Canadiens.

Herald, "How did these guys get into the playoffs?"

Hap Day, the Leaf coach, waved the quote at his players who operated in a fury in Game Two, winning 4–0. This was also the game in which Montreal's great scorer, Rocket Richard, grew so incensed at being flattened once too often by Ezinicki bodychecks that he conked Wild Bill over the head with his stick. The conk got Richard suspended for the next game. Toronto won the Rocket-less contest and took the following game on an overtime goal by Apps. The Canadiens won Game Five at the Montreal Forum, and the teams went back to the Gardens for the sixth game, which was tied 1–1 entering the third period.

"I had to reestablish myself as an NHLer," Ted Kennedy said many years later, speaking of the 1946–47 season. "I was goddarned determined. It was the same with Howie Meeker—he was just out of the armed services and desperate for a job."

So it seemed more than serendipity that at 14:39 of the third period, Meeker, the rookie and returned serviceman, fed a neat pass to Kennedy, the center coming off a previous season of injury and disappointment, who popped the goal that won the Stanley Cup.

What had begun for Conn Smythe in the spring of 1946 with several fits of pique ended a year later with a championship victory. And not, as things developed, just a single Stanley Cup, but three in a row and four in five years.

Howie Meeker was a wounded World War II vet when he joined the Leafs in the autumn of 1946. He stuck around for eight seasons and four Stanley Cups.

Smythe had created a mini-dynasty, and it was one large and audacious trade in November 1947 that put the Leafs in a position to keep on winning Cups. Toronto gave up five frontline players to the Chicago Black Hawks in return for Max Bentley, the center who was a dipsy-doodler on ice, Fred Astaire in skates, the most elusive of stickhandlers, the NHL's leading point scorer in each of the prior two seasons. Talk about strength down the middle: the Leafs had it with Apps, Kennedy and now Bentley playing the center position. The sportswriter Dick Beddoes once said altogether seriously that, on the Leaf team of 1947–48, Wayne Gretzky would have been the fourth center.

Splendid as Toronto was, the Leafs went into 1947–48's last weekend just a point in front of the tenacious Detroit Red Wings. But in a home-and-home pair of games that weekend—Saturday in Toronto and Sunday in Detroit—the Leafs won twice to wrap up first place. In the process of the two victories, Broda edged out Detroit's Harry Lumley for the Vezina Trophy, and Apps, who had already announced his retirement effective at the end of the season, scored five goals, which put him over 200 (201 to be exact) for his distinguished career.

The Leafs hardly paused for breath after such a blockbuster weekend. They knocked off the Boston Bruins in the Stanley Cup semifinals, four games to one, then rolled over the Red Wings in the finals in four straight. The Detroit series began with a couple of tense struggles at the Gardens, 5–3 and 4–2. Broda stoned the Red Wings 2–0 in the third game at the Detroit Olympia. Then, in Game Four, the Leafs put all the marvels of their season in one colossal outburst, overwhelming the helpless Wings on their home ice 7–2, capping the season for a group of players now almost unanimously celebrated as the best of all the Toronto teams.

Before the next season, to replace the retired Apps at center, Smythe traded with the New York Rangers to get Cal Gardner, a rangy guy with equal degrees of finesse and toughness. Alas, the addition of Gardner wasn't enough to keep the Leafs from sliding to

Captain Syl Apps's last hurrah in the NHL—he had already announced his retirement—came with a flourish when he lifted the Stanley Cup that his Leafs won at the end of the 1948 season.

Mr. Twinkle Toes on ice, a shifty skater and a master stickhandler, Max Bentley popped 245 goals in his NHL career and won three Stanley Cups with the Leafs.

OVERLEAF: Gallant in defeat—that was Detroit goalie Harry Lumley's role in the 1949 Stanley Cup finals. He played superbly, but it wasn't enough to save his Red Wings from losing in four straight to the red-hot Maple Leafs.

10

Detroit's Gordie Howe (right wing), Sid Abel (center) and Ted Lindsay (left wing) were called the Production Line, partly because the trio scored a grand total of 1,369 goals in their NHL lifetimes.

The player taking the nosedive is defenseman Bill Barilko, who had just slapped in the overtime goal that gave Toronto the 1951 Stanley Cup win over Montreal.

Bill Barilko was riding high after he scored the goal that won Toronto's 1951 Stanley Cup, but a few months later, the small plane he and a friend were flying across northern Ontario crashed into the wilderness killing both men.

fourth place in the season standings. "But none of us players worried about bein' in fourth," Howie Meeker said years afterward. "We knew we'd come out smellin' sweet." And so they did. In the playoffs, Toronto once again clipped Boston in five games in the semifinals, and once again blitzed the Red Wings in four straight in the finals. And who scored the winning goal against Detroit in Game Four, the goal that gave the Leafs their third straight Stanley Cup? None other than Cal Gardner.

Jack Adams was getting irked over Detroit's losses to Toronto in these final series, two blowouts in two years. Adams, whose fuse was

Don Simmons's stop on this point-blank blast from Rocket Richard didn't prevent the Canadiens from winning the 1957 Cup over the Boston Bruins.

Jacques Plante stayed firm in resisting a shot from Toronto's George Armstrong as Plante's Canadiens took the 1959 Cup final.

even shorter than Conn Smythe's, had been the Red Wings' general manager since 1928. He was something of a hockey genius, generally credited with inventing the game's farm system in which young players were groomed to play for the big team. The system helped to produce for the Red Wings what was probably the single best forward line in the NHL, young Gordie Howe at right wing, equally young Ted Lindsay on the left side and wily old Sid Abel at center. But even with these wizards, Detroit couldn't beat the infernal Leafs, and Adams resolved that the 1949–50 season would be different.

Events seemed to proceed according to the Adams plan. Detroit finished the season in first place by eleven points, and the "Production Line," as Howe-Lindsay-Abel were known, ended one-two-three in scoring (Lindsay first, then Abel, then Howe). But in the third period of the first game of the playoff semifinals against Toronto, Detroit was struck by what seemed the ultimate disaster. Howe, trying to check Ted Kennedy, lost his balance, crashed into the boards and fell to the ice in a bleeding, broken heap. He had sustained fractured bones in his face and a fracture to his skull,

Gerry McNeil, making like a Russian dancer, took this shot on his toe in 1951 Cup play, but his Canadiens lost out to the Leafs in the finals.

Jacques Plante juggled the puck on the way to five straight Montreal Stanley Cups including this one in 1959 over the Leafs.

The 1954 Red Wings, captained by the rugged left winger Ted Lindsay (center), won the Cup in a close seven-game series against the Canadiens.

The Red Wings caught another break at Montreal's expense in the following season. This run of Detroit luck began, perversely, with a riot. In mid-March of the season, 1954–55, the tempestuous Maurice Richard lost his cool in a game at the Boston Garden. He used his fists and stick to flatten a Bruins player, Hal Laycoe. Not quite finished with the haymakers, the Rocket also bopped a linesman, Cliff Thompson. NHL president Clarence Campbell, bringing his version of swift justice to the matter, suspended Richard for the rest of the season, a sentence that incredibly included the whole of the upcoming playoffs. The suspension outraged all of Montreal, where it was suspected that the very English Campbell was acting from an anti-French Quebec motive, and a few days later at the Canadiens' next home game on St. Patrick's Day night, the

Maurice "Rocket" Richard, his younger, smaller brother Henri, the "Pocket Rocket" and Dickie "No Nickname" Moore supplied much of the goal power for the 1956 Canadiens, who won the first of Montreal's five straight Stanley Cups.

These four members of the 1955 Canadiens put plenty of rubber in the net: left to right, Bernie "Boom Boom" Geoffrion, Rocket Richard, Jean Beliveau and Kenny Mosdell.

fans in the Montreal Forum were primed for demonstrative action. Campbell gave them an excuse to detonate when, either from an excess of chutzpah or ignorance, he showed up in person at the Forum. At the end of the first period, fans tossed programs in Campbell's direction, hot dogs, galoshes, anything that came to hand. Someone—possibly a Montreal policeman—unleashed a canister of tear gas inside the Forum, and the riot was on.

Among the casualties of the violence was that night's game,

which was forfeited to the visiting team. This happened to be Detroit, and even though the Red Wings were leading Montreal 4–1 at the time of the forfeiture, they welcomed the automatic two points. When the season ended two games later, Detroit emerged in first place over Montreal by a margin of—oh, terrible irony—two points. That gave the Red Wings home-ice advantage throughout the playoffs, a fact of hockey life that came into significant play when the Stanley Cup finals were ultimately decided in a seventh game, Detroit versus Montreal. At home in the Olympia on the night of that contest, everything went according to comfortable form for the Red Wings. Pete and Jerry Cusimano flung an octopus on to the ice, Alex Delvecchio scored twice and Detroit won 3–1 to capture its second straight Stanley Cup.

Jack Adams and the other people and players in the Red Wings organization anticipated many more Cups to follow. But their optimism was doomed to nightmarish disappointment because the next championship team from Detroit didn't materialize for decades, not until 1997, which was about the time Delvecchio began to draw his old-age pension. What derailed the Red Wings' immediate expectations for additional Stanley Cups in the mid-1950s was the emergence in Montreal, arising out of the debacle of the Richard riot, of a Canadiens team that dominated the NHL in a fashion unaccomplished before 1956 and unequaled after 1960. In the space of those five years, Montreal, astoundingly, won the maximum of five Stanley Cups.

This was the Montreal team of veterans, and of kids almost young enough to be the veterans' children—or at least their younger brothers. It was the team of thirty-five-year-old Rocket Richard entering his glorious final seasons and of his nineteen-year-old sibling, Henri, embarking on his precocious early seasons. It was the team of Doug Harvey who had arrived with the Canadiens in 1947–48 as a raw recruit from Montreal's west end, and who grew so polished and crafty that, beginning in 1954–55, he won seven out of the next eight Norris Trophies for best defenseman in the league. It was the team of Tom Johnson, a clever and disciplined defender who joined the team from Winnipeg in the year after Harvey's debut and won the Norris in the one year of the eight that Harvey didn't win it. It was the team of a goalie, Jacques Plante, who was part

Perhaps the most elegant player of his era, Jean Beliveau scored 507 goals in his twenty NHL years, all with Montreal.

eccentric (he knitted toques for a hobby), part visionary (he pioneered the protective face mask for goalies) and all All-Star (he won the Vezina Trophy in each of the five consecutive Stanley Cup seasons). And it was the team of forwards who had grown to early maturity playing with and against one another in the Quebec junior leagues: the elegant Jean Beliveau from Victoriaville, the intrepid Dickie Moore of the Montreal Junior Canadiens, the boisterous Bernie "Boom Boom" Geoffrion from the Montreal-based Junior Nationales. It was the team built in all its ingredients for the long haul of Stanley Cups.

Perhaps most of all, it was the team of Frank Selke, the very fellow whom Conn Smythe had ushered so peremptorily out of Maple Leaf Gardens in the spring of 1946. The Canadiens scooped up Selke as its managing director within weeks of his departure from the Leafs. He was fifty-three at the time, a short, anonymous-looking man with an avuncular air and an insistence on the loftiest standards in his professional field, which was organizing hockey teams, and in his avocational interest, which was raising specially bred chickens and pigeons. Selke was a master at picking hockey talent and grooming it for tenure with the Canadiens. Of the significant members of the five consecutive Stanley Cup teams, all except two—Beliveau and the winger who handled all the digging for the puck on Rocket's line, Bert Olmstead—came out of the Montreal farm system. And, in another statistic illustrating the thoroughness of Selke's team building, no fewer than twelve players, from Plante to Harvey to Moore and not excluding the amazing Rocket, starred on all five of Montreal's historic Cup winners.

Toe Blake delivered the goods for Montreal as a player on the ice, then went behind the bench and coached the team to eight Stanley Cups.

Paradoxically, Selke's key move in getting his dynasty of the late 1950s under way had nothing to do with choosing players and everything to do with changing coaches. Dick Irvin, coach of the Canadiens for more than a decade, had grown truculent on the job. Selke wanted someone to apply a calmer hand to the team, a man who combined Irvin's admitted hockey smarts with a quieter brand of authority. He put the call out to Toe Blake, the former All-Star left winger for the Canadiens, and a coach who had been learning the nuances of the craft in the Quebec senior league and the American Hockey League. Blake went behind the Montreal bench and turned out to be precisely what Dr. Selke ordered.

"The guy knew how to prime you for a game," Plante said of Blake. "He knew what button to push to get the most out of guys because he always wanted to maintain the edge."

Blake pushed enough buttons in his rookie coaching year, 1955–56, to carry the Canadiens to a colossal twenty-four-point lead over second-place Detroit in the regular season's final standings. The NHL was all Montreal, all the time, all year. Beliveau led the league in total goals and assists. Four Canadiens—Plante, Harvey, Beliveau and the Rocket—made the First All-Star Team, and two more—Johnson and Olmstead—made the Second. In hardware, the team cleaned up: the Vezina for Plante, Norris for Harvey, Hart for Beliveau. This Montreal team presented the total hockey package, and while Detroit struggled valiantly against the Canadiens in the

EXIT

Goalie Johnny Bower and his Leaf teammates may have had Montreal under control in this 1959 playoff photo, but it was the Canadiens who prevailed over Toronto in the Cup finals.

10

Stanley Cup finals, managing to win one game, Montreal virtually breezed through the series, Beliveau leading the way by scoring seven of his team's total of eighteen goals.

The principal change in the Canadiens the following season lay in the crowning of a new team captain. The respected defenseman Butch Bouchard retired that year and left the captaincy vacant. With Bouchard's departure, the mantle of team captain, in an organization where such things were treated with the same gravity as the selection of a pope, passed to the next most senior Canadien who happened to be Maurice Richard. To outsiders, the Rocket seemed too combustible for such a role. The nutcase who socked linesmen and precipitated riots? Surely not. His teammates saw things differently. To them, the Rocket was the man who stalked the dressing room after a Montreal loss, leveling his famous glare on fellow players, saying little but communicating the message that defeat did not become his team. It was leadership by intimidation, and the other Canadiens thrived on it.

Richard similarly led in the arena, especially at playoff time. In the Stanley Cup finals against Boston in the first year of his captaincy, 1956–57, the Rocket set the pace in the opening game by scoring four goals in Montreal's 5–1 win. Then Richard stepped aside while Jacques Plante and the defensemen took over, allowing the Bruins a non-threatening six goals in the five games the series lasted. That made two Stanley Cups in two years for Montreal.

Number three in the next season also owed much to Richard. What made his performance particularly remarkable was that, earlier in the year, his career appeared to have been forever canceled. In a November game against Toronto, Leaf defenseman Marc Reaume's skate blade sliced into Richard's tendon. The Rocket, hobbled and not in the flush of youth at thirty-seven, was nevertheless back on skates by February, and in the playoffs, it was he who saved Montreal's bacon. In the semifinals against Detroit, the Canadiens were up two games to one, but in the fourth game, the Red Wings led 3–1, and seemed a cinch to tie the series and seize the momentum. Richard interpreted the situation as a signal to go into goal-scoring mode, and he didn't quit until he had a hat trick, which paved the way for a Canadiens win in the series. Again, in the finals

against Boston, the Rocket produced a key goal, an overtime score in the fifth game that put Montreal on course to take another Stanley Cup, the ultimate Cup-winning goal coming on a typically authoritative shot by Boom Boom Geoffrion.

The following year, 1958–59, when the Canadiens once more reached the Cup finals, they found an unexpected opponent waiting for them: the Toronto Maple Leafs. Before the season began, Toronto had hired a new general manager to rescue the team from a decade of lousy hockey. The savior was a veteran of minor-league management, Punch Imlach, and in one of his early moves, Imlach appointed a new coach—himself. But the players failed to respond to the Imlach approach until only nine days remained in the season and the Leafs were stuck at seven points out of the last playoff spot. At this instant of crisis, the team went on a tear, winning five straight games to edge out the New York Rangers for fourth place by a single point, then knocking off the Bruins in the Cup semifinals.

Which was when the Canadiens broke Leaf hearts. The finals lasted only five games, but each qualified as a struggle, two games decided by one goal, the other three by two. And Montreal benefited from a large piece of bizarre luck. In Game Four at the Gardens, the Leafs' George Armstrong let blast with a shot that appeared to zip past Jacques Plante and into the Montreal net. In fact, it apparently kept on zipping through a flaw in the netting and out the other side. The Leafs and viewing audience saw it as a goal. The referee didn't. He prevailed. The game ended 3–2 for the Canadiens who proceeded to their fourth Stanley Cup in a row.

Montreal needed nothing as trifling as a fortunate break in 1959–60. It was a season when the only thing that might have gone wrong for the Canadiens happened in a game on November 1, 1959. Andy Bathgate of the New York Rangers banked a shot off Plante's chin. Plante gushed blood. A doctor sewed seven stitches to close the wound. Plante, fed up with years of taking pucks in the kisser, reached for the newfangled piece of equipment he'd been experimenting with in practice. So it was that the goalie mask made its debut in the NHL. Plante and the mask kept on stopping pucks all season, and in the Stanley Cup finals, goalie and mask got really hot. In the four games it took Montreal to eliminate the Leafs (the Canadiens had also used the minimum four in brushing aside

Butch Bouchard, Montreal's rock solid defenseman for fifteen seasons, brought a laugh to his work when he helped the Canadiens to a 1956 Stanley Cup win.

Andy Bathgate, smart and stylish with the Rangers, finally won his first and only Stanley Cup when he joined the Leafs in 1964. Here he poses for his official hockey card photo. The field in the background would be removed from the photo before the final card was made.

The Black Hawks, the NHL's sad sack for decades, woke up in the early 1960s when Pierre Pilote gave them smarts on the blue line.

In 1961, Glenn Hall backstopped Chicago to its first Stanley Cup in twenty-three seasons.

Chicago in the semifinals), Plante plus mask allowed only five goals. "This," Frank Selke said of Plante and his teammates on that year's Canadiens, "is the best of all Montreal teams."

Selke and the rest of his organization knew that their unprecedented streak of Cups must eventually come to an end. What surprised the Canadiens was the identity of the team that put the stopper to them. It was the perpetually terrible Chicago Black Hawks. Chicago had been the league doormat since the 1938 season, finishing last more times (ten) in the following couple of decades than it finished first or second (never). By the late 1950s, the owners of the other five NHL teams recognized that it wasn't good business to operate the league with such a pathetically have-not team, given the attendant loss of fan interest and arena revenue in Chicago. The five adopted a deliberate policy of propping up the Hawks by delivering to them, by trade or sale, players who were not mere castoffs. Thus, Chicago got the iron man of goalies, Glenn Hall, from Detroit; the hard-nosed forward, Eric Nesterenko, from Toronto; and, among a half-dozen other useful commodities from Montreal, the towering defenseman, Dollard St. Laurent. At the same time, Chicago's formerly lame farm system rewarded the Hawks with two authentic superstars: Bobby Hull, "Mr. Slap Shot," and Stan Mikita, no slouch as a goal scorer and a supremely disciplined center.

Of all the qualities the Black Hawks now boasted, it was their toughness that most benefited them at Stanley Cup time. When first-place Montreal met the third-place Hawks in the Cup semifinals of 1960–61, the Canadiens fully expected to encounter a ferocious defense. After all, Hall had allowed fewer goals in the regular season than their own Plante. But Montreal hadn't counted on the bruising nature of all the hard-hitting characters in the Chicago lineup, guys like Nesterenko, St. Laurent, Pierre Pilote and Elmer "Moose" Vasko (the latter two from the flourishing farm system). The Hawks prevailed on muscle in those semifinals, and in the finals, they dished out more of the same brawn to Detroit. The Red Wings matched the Hawks check for check in the first four games, but with the series tied at two wins apiece, Chicago reached for more beef than Detroit could equal, and the Hawks rolled over the subdued Wings in scores unusual in the tradition of the finals

Stan Mikita (with 541 lifetime goals) and Bobby Hull (with 610) handled most of the offense for the winning Chicago teams of the 1960s.

OVERLEAF: Chicago's Glenn Hall deflected this shot from Toronto's George Armstrong in the 1962 finals, but the Leafs popped enough goals behind Hall to capture the Cup.

EXIT

Clear the track, here comes Toronto's Eddie Shack, right past Hawks' goalie Glenn Hall in the 1962 final series, won by the Leafs.

for the decisiveness of their margin, 6–3 and 5–1. Chicago had its first Stanley Cup in twenty-three years.

The Hawks returned to the finals the following season, this time against the Maple Leafs, a team that was built on experience and guile. From among the players Punch Imlach inherited when he joined Toronto, he kept those who were long on NHL service and hockey intelligence. He added a few more of the same types through trades; notable among them was Red Kelly, Detroit's veteran star defenseman whom Imlach, in an inspired adjustment, converted to a star center. Imlach's tinkering gave the Leafs a collection of smart senior citizens who included defensemen Allan Stanley (entering NHL season number thirteen), Tim Horton (twelve) and Larry Hillman (seven), and, up front, Kelly (fourteen) and George

Things got so nasty between the Black Hawks and the Leafs in the 1962 Cup finals that it was standing room only in the penalty box.

Johnny Bower, on his feet or his knees, was the final line of defense for four Toronto Stanley Cup teams in the 1960s.

Armstrong (twelve). Even the young guys on the Leafs were players with lofty hockey IQs: the perfect little center Dave Keon and the ever-resourceful winger Dick Duff. In goal, Toronto depended on the Satchel Paige of hockey, Johnny Bower, who may have been thirty-five years old or more likely forty-five or maybe 105.

In the finals between this brainy bunch and the Hawks, the outcome turned on two major events. The first came in the opening period of Game Four, the Leafs leading the series two games to one. Hull unleashed one of his faster-than-a-speeding-bullet slap shots at the Toronto net. Bower did the splits to make the save, but in the process, he pulled the hamstring muscle in his left leg. The pull put him out of commission for the rest of the playoffs. Don Simmons, the backup goalie, took over. Was Simmons up to the challenge? Not immediately. Chicago took the game 4–1 to square the series.

But in Game Five, Simmons buckled down, and the Leafs got the

Defenseman Bobby Baun wrapped up the Cup for the Leafs in 1963.

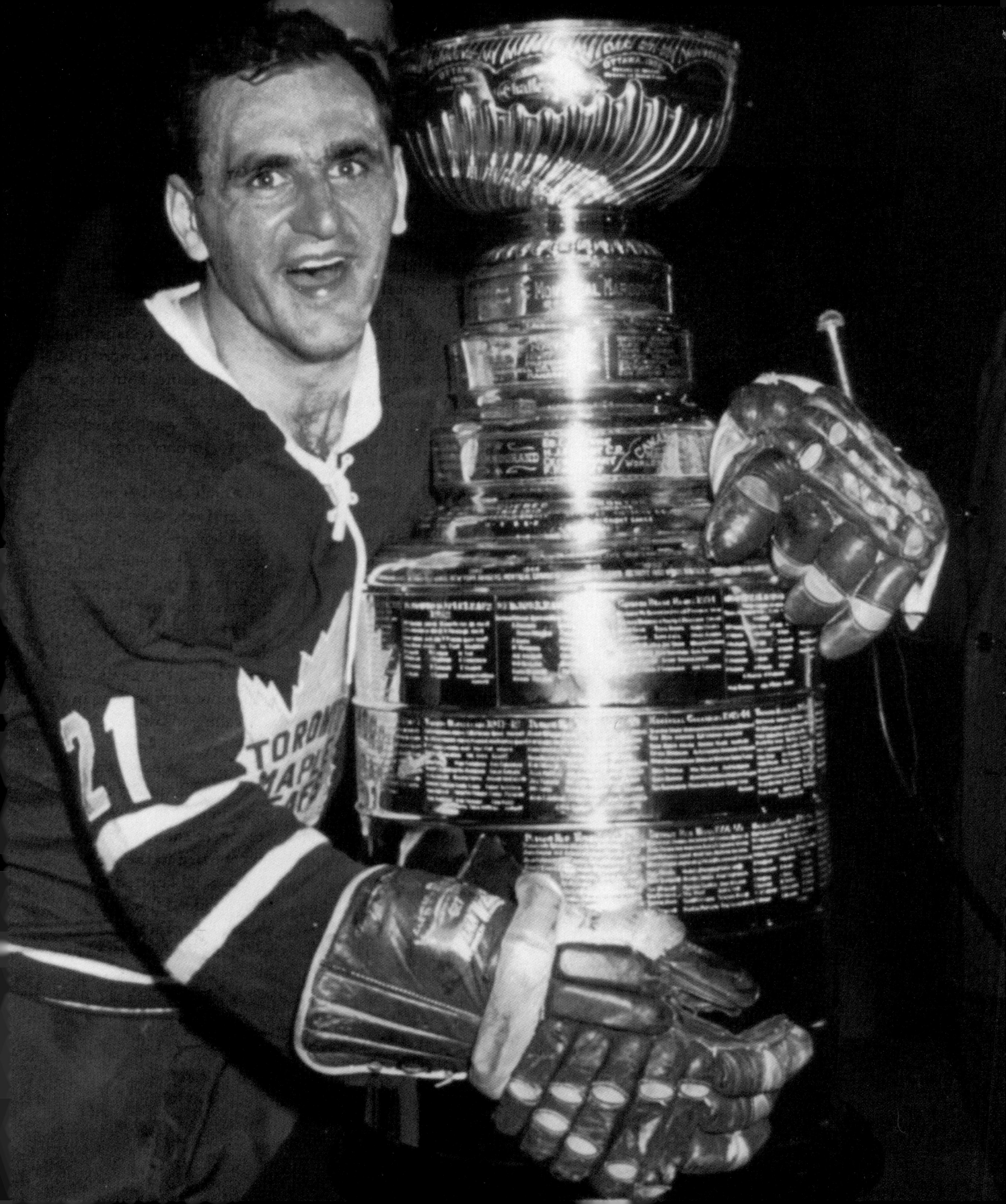
21

Red Kelly pulled off a remarkable double: star defenseman for Detroit and star center for the Leafs, helping to win Stanley Cups for both teams.

win, which established the circumstances for the second major event in Game Six at the Chicago Stadium. Halfway through the third period, with things tied 0–0, Hull whipped a shot past Simmons for the go-ahead goal. The Hawks fans whooped, screamed, cheered and tossed stuff on the ice. The celebration, especially the tossing-stuff-on-the-ice part, delayed the game by fifteen minutes. During the long time-out, the Hawk players cooled off. The more seasoned Leafs took the opportunity to reclaim their focus, and ninety seconds after play resumed, Toronto winger Bob Nevin, another smart operator, scored to tie the game. Four minutes after that, Horton rushed the puck across the Leaf blue line and into the Chicago zone. He passed to an open Duff who banged in the goal that brought the Stanley Cup back to Toronto after an eleven-year absence.

The Leafs liked the feeling of victory so much that they won the Cup again the next season. In that year's semifinals, they breezed past Montreal in five games, outscoring the Canadiens fourteen goals to six. The old Leaf guys were sizzling, and they kept up the sizzle against Detroit in the finals, once more winning four games to one. It was Keon who performed the big offensive feats. He got the winning goal in Game Four, and in Game Five, a 3–1 Leafs victory, Wee Davey popped two of the three goals.

In the 1963–64 finals, a Toronto-Detroit repeat, the Leafs benefited from a guy with a broken foot. Toronto kept trailing in the series, down two games to one, then three games to two. In the third period of Game Six at the Olympia, tied at 3–3, Leaf defenseman Bob Baun took a zinger of an Alex Delvecchio shot off the ankle. The Leaf doctor suspected a hairline fracture of the fibula. Baun, a man with the build, looks and imperturbability of a small, craggy mountain, begged the doc to freeze the foot. The doc obliged, and in the overtime period, Baun returned to the ice and scored on a shot from the point. The series was all knotted up, and in the seventh game, Baun, whose fibula was indeed fractured, played again with freezing treatment. So did three other Leafs—the heady defenseman Carl Brewer (separated ribs), Kelly (twisted knee ligaments) and Armstrong (separated shoulder). The wounded guys triumphed, Kelly even managing to score a goal, and with the 4–0 win, Toronto had its third consecutive Stanley Cup.

In the last game of the 1964 Cup finals, Leaf Captain George Armstrong played with freezing treatment in his separated shoulder, but a few days later, he felt fit enough to carry the Stanley Cup through Toronto's jubilant streets.

OVERLEAF: The puck trickled just too far for Detroit goalie Roger Crozier to reach, a cruel fate that happened often enough to give Montreal the Cup in the 1966 finals.

24
20

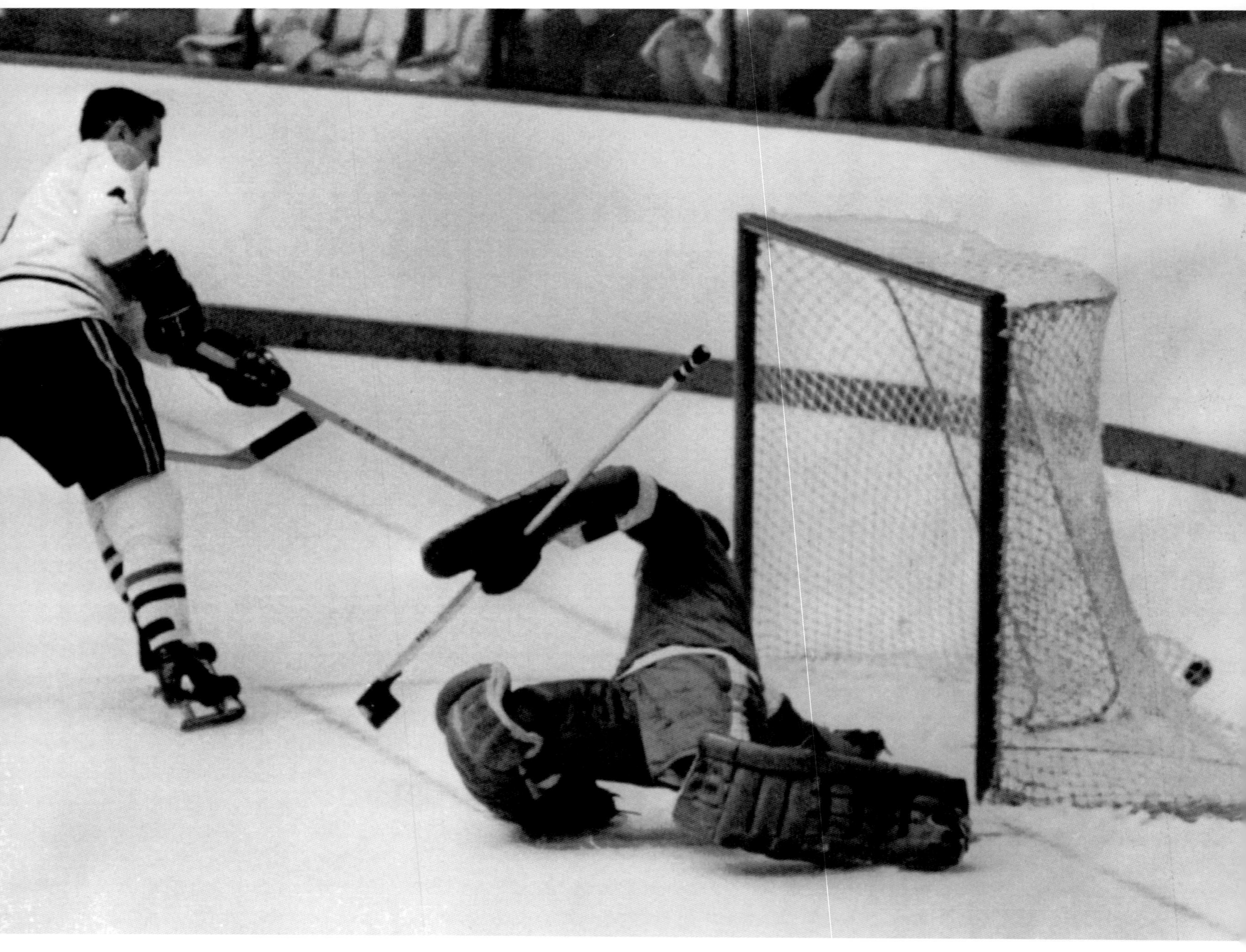

Jean Beliveau, all alone in front of the Red Wings' Roger Crozier, scored a goal that helped make Beliveau the 1966 playoff MVP, and Montreal the Stanley Cup champs.

It was the Canadiens who prevented the Leafs from making it four straight. This Montreal team presented a vastly different look from the stylish outfit that dazzled its way to Stanley Cups a few years earlier. Among the skill forwards, big Jean Beliveau was still around, and so was little Henri Richard, "the Pocket Rocket," who had entered the most inventive phase of his career. But the backbone of the team consisted of some large, powerful, inelegant defensemen—Ted Harris, Terry Harper, Jacques Laperriere—and a mean and muscular forward, John Ferguson, who was ever ready to

The Leafs' Bob Pulford showed his tap dancing form to celebrate the winning goal he scored against Montreal in the final game of the 1967 playoffs.

put up his dukes. It was these strong men, foreign to coach Toe Blake's earlier teams, who guaranteed that Beliveau, the Pocket Rocket and Montreal's other smallish forwards could make their offensive moves in relative peace.

Blake guided this mix-and-match bunch with his usual canny instinct. Among his other coachly attributes, Blake seemed always to think a half step ahead of his rivals, to put players on the ice in combinations that gave his Canadiens the edge. This talent was on particular display in the Stanley Cup finals, Montreal (who eliminated Toronto in the semis) versus Chicago. The Hawks still relied on Bobby Hull plus brawn, but now Blake had the answers with his own burly defensemen. The series turned predictably into a brutal war, a battle of gladiators that Montreal won in seven games for two principal reasons. One was that their big guys outlasted Chicago's, and the other was that Beliveau came up huge, scoring sixteen points in the playoffs and winning the first ever Conn Smythe Trophy awarded to the Stanley Cup MVP.

Blake's quick thinking figured into the Cup finals a year later, in 1965–66, when the Canadiens met the Red Wings. Montreal led three games to two going into the Olympia for Game Six. At the end of regulation time, the score was tied at 2–2. In overtime, the Pocket Rocket took the puck and flew in on Roger Crozier who had been sensational in the Detroit net throughout the series. Richard fell. But as he slid along the ice, so did the puck. It ended its slide in the net. But had the puck been carried on the Pocket Rocket's stick, which would make it the Cup-winning goal, or had it been

Toronto's George Armstrong and Montreal's Serge Savard compared shoulders in the 1967 playoffs when the Leafs outmuscled the Canadiens for the Cup.

Frank Mahovlich of the Leafs went eye to eye with Gump Worsley in the 1967 finals, but on this rush the Gumper didn't blink.

carried by Richard's body, which would make it a non-goal? The instant reaction of everybody in the arena was to look to referee Frank Udvari for his signal. That wasn't Blake's response. Before Udvari could move an arm, Blake sent his bench players spilling on the ice in celebration. Udvari made no signal. Maybe, in fact, he had no chance to make a signal. Either way, Montreal went home with the Stanley Cup.

The next season, 1966–67, should have belonged to the Black Hawks. They finished the regular season in first place, seventeen points in front of runner-up Montreal; Stan Mikita led the league in total points, and Hull scored more goals in a single season than any player before him in NHL history, 52. But in the Stanley Cup semifinals, the Hawks were stymied by Toronto's alternating

MAPLE
LEAFS
18
CUSTOM
PRO.
VICTORIAVILLE PRO-

Yvan Cournoyer of the Canadiens got some distance on the Leafs' Marcel Pronovost, an event that didn't happen frequently in Toronto's 1967 Cup victory.

Jean-Claude Tremblay was one of many Canadiens who couldn't catch Toronto's Dave Keon on his way to playoff MVP in 1967.

goaltenders, Johnny Bower and Terry Sawchuk, and the Leafs' win matched them against Montreal in the finals.

The Toronto team was positively geriatric, a gang of codgers. Two key players topped forty years, Bower and Stanley, and all the others were sufficiently advanced in years that the team's age averaged out to an ancient 31.4. But with the years, the Leafs had acquired such other qualities as steadfastness and mental toughness largely unknown to younger players. In the words of Marcel Pronovost, Toronto's defenseman (age thirty-six), "We don't get nervous." In the Montreal series, though one of the kids of the group, twenty-six-year-old Dave Keon, was the sublime star, the old lads played unflappable hockey. In Game Three, Bower stopped fifty-two Montreal shots and Toronto won in double overtime. And in Game Six, with Toronto leading the series three games to two, Kelly set up the first goal, Armstrong scored another, Sawchuk allowed only a single Montreal goal and the Leafs became the oldest team ever to win the Stanley Cup.

In retrospect, it was a bittersweet victory for Toronto. Before the season began, Conn Smythe, the man who had inaugurated the Leafs' postwar string of excellence more than two decades earlier, severed his ties with the Gardens. Some of the excellence must have gone with him because, after 1966–67, the Leafs didn't win another Stanley Cup, nor even reach the finals, during the rest of the twentieth century.

Day of the Dynasties 1968–1983

Paul Henderson's heroics in the historic 1972 summit series against the Russians set the stage for many changes on the hockey landscape.

May 1968: student riots break out in Paris and spread around the world. Once cuddly Beatle John Lennon and girlfriend Yoko Ono are busted for pot. Trudeaumania flowers (due to the popularity of Canada's prime minister) and man blasts off for the moon. You say you want a revolution?

The National Hockey League was not immune to these forces of change. Hair became longer and so did the schedule as the league multiplied from six to twelve to twenty-one teams by the end of the next decade. Bobby Orr blazed a trail that Wayne Gretzky eventually followed.

The 1972 Canada-Russia series changed the game on both sides of the Atlantic, but not where fighting and intimidation were concerned. Once an honorable way for the players to police themselves, a dark age gave birth to the goon, and fisticuffs became a tactic for the future Big Bad Bruins and the Broad Street Bullies.

But as the hockey world became bigger and nastier, the roll call of Cup winners did not. Between 1968 and 1983, the silverware changed hands just four times. The Montreal Canadiens adapted to the shifting climates and spread eight Cups between 1968 and 1979. Boston and Philadelphia were each two-time winners and appeared in a total of seven finals. Then came the New York Islanders, entering the eighties with four straight titles.

"As in baseball, dynasties were great, unless you grew up outside of New York and didn't like the Yankees," said Ken Dryden, who backed the Habs to six titles and is now president of the Maple Leafs. "It wasn't much fun for anyone else.

"The good thing about having a few teams dominate is that it's a standard to chase. But you need the right standards. Montreal played a way you'd think everyone would try and replicate.

"The Canadiens [in Dryden's day] didn't just win, they dominated. They gave you no breathing room, no crack in their armor and never a sense that there would be a crack. But you never

Ralph Backstrom of the Canadiens tests St. Louis netminder Glenn Hall as Blues' defenseman Barclay Plager gives chase. This was the first Cup final involving an expansion team.

The NHL playoffs became a twelve-team tournament in 1968, but the Montreal Canadiens were very familiar posing with Lord Stanley's mug after beating the Blues.

Hall won the Conn Smythe Trophy in a losing cause in 1968 and came back to face the mighty Habs in the 1969 finals.

Lorne (Gump) Worsley had a 1.73 goals against average in the sweep of the Blues in 1968. Here, he denied Red Berenson.

VICTORIAVILLE

Jacques Lemaire, seen here in the early 1970s, was a member of eight Stanley Cup winning teams in Montreal. From 1993–1998 he was coach of the New Jersey Devils and led the team to a surprising four game sweep of Detroit in the 1995 Stanley Cup finals.

felt you could depend on destiny. You had to create it."

On May 5, 1968, the St. Louis Blues tried just that. They became the first non-Original Six club in thirty-three years to play a Cup final game. They couldn't have drawn a tougher foe, with coach Toe Blake's Canadiens sworn to atone for losing to the Leafs the previous spring.

The Blues were led by a young desert fox named Scotty Bowman, who had coached the junior Canadiens, with a Montreal Forum office down the hall from Blake. Bowman, destined to become the winningest coach in league history, would often refer to his rookie year in St. Louis as his finest. He took a team that included seven players thirty-five or older into the playoffs, through two seven-game series, and one game of double overtime.

"We had quite a bit of confidence in that final," Bowman said. "We were strong in goal with Glenn Hall and fortunately, our farm team in Kansas City was eliminated, so we had [Kansas City player-coach] Doug Harvey up. Al Arbour was hurt, but he somehow got into the seventh game [against the North Stars] and was ready for the final. Jean Beliveau was hurt for them going into that series, so we were as high as we could be."

Harvey, Dickie Moore and Hall had forty years of playoff experience, but Blake's team was incredibly balanced. The Canadiens had 236 goals without a top ten scorer, six players who'd won trophies or were runners-up, and two All-Stars in Gump Worsely and J. C. Tremblay. Blessed with home-ice advantage under the first year of a rotating format, the Blues held a 2–1 lead late in the second period on goals by Barclay Plager and Moore. But it would be their pinnacle in the series. Yvan Cournoyer forced overtime and an unassisted Jacques Lemaire goal 1:41 into overtime avoided an upset in the seventy-four-shot game.

The St. Louis Arena was rocking again in Game Two as Worsley and Hall dueled into a scoreless third. But rookie defenseman Serge Savard scored the first of his two shorthanded goals in the series. Hall, en route to the Conn Smythe Trophy, was blitzed in Game Three, 46–15 on the shot clock, but Dick Duff set up Bobby Rousseau in overtime for a 4–3 win. Another dogged Blues effort in Game Four ended with Tremblay potting a goal and adding an assist in a 3–2 clincher. With his eighth Cup in thirteen years as a coach, and three more as a player, Blake stepped down.

"We knew before the series that he was going to retire," Bowman said. "Being eliminated was tough and being swept was even more difficult. But over the years, knowing that it was his last one, it's softened the memory a little bit."

Claude Ruel inherited Blake's job, just the third coaching change in Montreal in twenty-eight years. Bowing to growing nationalist sentiments in Quebec, Sam Pollock chose a francophone. But it made little difference on the ice as the team compiled a then-record

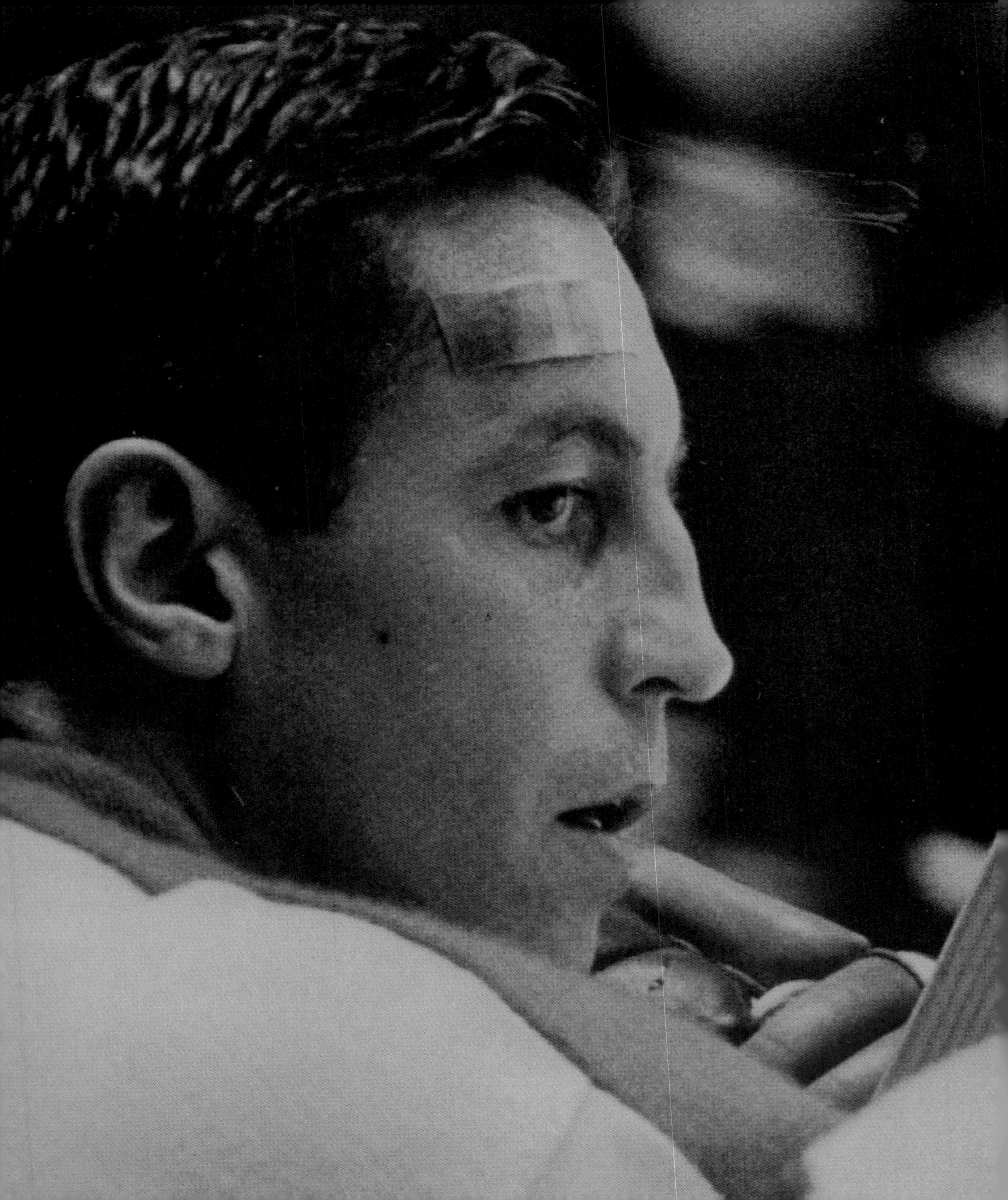

Revered Canadiens' captain Jean Beliveau collected 176 playoff points before going out as a Stanley Cup champion in 1971 against Chicago. He won his first Cup in 1956.

103 points and drew the Blues in the finals again. Like Montreal, they'd barely altered their lineup.

Former Hab great Jacques Plante opposed young Rogie Vachon in the opener, but the latter earned a 3–1 win. Hall returned the next game, but St. Louis would get just one even-strength goal the rest of the series, losing 3–1, 4–0, 2–1. Savard, who was used partly as a forward, became the first rookie to win the Smythe, while Ruel was the eleventh newcomer to take his team to the title.

"We had great teams in St. Louis," Bowman lamented. "Despite the scores in the finals, we were really close."

The two Canadian-based teams had carved the Cup between them since 1962, but a formidable machine from Massachusetts now threatened the monopoly. For three years, the Bruins had led the league in offense and now Orr entered the 1970 playoffs as the first 100-point defenseman. The Bruins came out of a twenty-nine-year Cup hibernation in a grouchy mood, blasting the Black Hawks and Rangers to meet the Blues, the only club in the West with a winning record that year. Orr presented a daunting problem.

"We tried to shadow Bobby with another defenseman, Jimmy Roberts, something I don't think had been tried before," Bowman said. "Orr had just that one goal [the Cup winner], but it was Johnny Bucyk and those other guys who went wild against us."

Bucyk's Game One hat trick quickly robbed St. Louis of home-ice advantage, while Orr had two first-period assists in the 6–2 second-game romp that followed. Orr, providing one of the most famous hockey pictures of all time, sailed through the air in overtime of Game Four, after directing Derek Sanderson's puck past Hall.

"A spectacular goal by a spectacular player," Bruins coach Harry Sinden said. Orr gambled on that play to keep the puck in deep.

"It might have turned out differently if he'd been caught," Bowman said ruefully. Sinden, who likes to needle, disagreed.

"We have still photographs that showed Ed Westfall was covering for Bobby, as any well-coached team would," he said with a laugh.

Boston's plans to repeat were thwarted by a cerebral six-foot-four-inch law student, who was on the farm team in Halifax, Nova Scotia, until March of 1971.

"I arrived at the airport in Montreal the same moment the Canadiens flew back from a game," Dryden said. "They were all

OVERLEAF: Glenn Hall knew Derek Sanderson and the Boston Bruins were hungry for the Cup in 1970 and the unfortunate Blues were no match in a four-game sweep, the third straight time they were swept.

16
17

30
20

looking at me and wondering, 'Who is he and what is he doing here?'"

Dryden knew the Boston Garden well from raucous ECAC games with Cornell. He also played in the Chicago Stadium during one of his six regular-season games, and both experiences served him well in the playoffs.

"I made some terrific discoveries, namely that teams play better defense in the playoffs and that I could play amidst the excitement," Dryden said.

The Canadiens survived a seven-game quarterfinal against the Bruins, after they were down 3–2. After getting by the Stars, they faced a balanced Chicago team that still boasted Bobby and Dennis Hull and Stan Mikita up front.

Chicago rained almost 100 shots on Dryden in the first two games, as a 2–1 overtime winner by Jim Pappin and a four-point game by Lou Angotti put Montreal in a quick 2–0 series hole. But Frank and Pete Mahovlich, reunited at mid-season, and the proud Beliveau with the last of his 176 playoff points pulled them even. Then it was Tony Esposito's turn to shine, blanking all thirty-one Habs shots in Game Five.

"Losing that one was a real shocker," Dryden said. "Henri Richard was benched that game. People around the city started muttering that [coach] Al MacNeil was incompetent and we began to hear about death threats against him. It seemed we were disintegrating, but it never got that far."

Frank Mahovlich, who would

Goaltender Gerry Cheevers and friends show the Blues in 1970 that the Bruins were much more than just Bobby Orr and Phil Esposito.

The Big Bad Bruins' 1970 title was their first in twenty-nine years. Bobby Orr celebrates in the victors' dressing room.

The Black Hawks took Montreal to seven games in 1971, but Bobby Hull finds it difficult to beat Jacques Laperriere (left), Guy Lapointe (right) and Ken Dryden in goal.

eventually tie Phil Esposito's record of twenty-seven points, was in on two power play goals in a 4–3 Forum win. Mahovlich missed a penalty shot on Tony O to open Game Seven as Montreal fell behind by a pair. But a Lemaire rush put the Canadiens on the board, giving way to two Richard goals, the winner coming early in the third.

Dryden, the unlikely hero, was awarded the Smythe, a year before he played enough games to qualify for his rookie of the year prize.

Bobby Orr beats Glenn Hall for the overtime goal that completes Boston sweep of St. Louis in 1970.

A wiser Boston club saved some energy for 1972, routing the Leafs and Blues to set up their first Cup final against the Rangers in forty-three years. New York had finished second to Boston in the regular season, with Jean Ratelle, Vic Hadfield and Rod Gilbert shadowing Orr and Esposito in the scoring race.

Rangers defenseman Harry Howell, the last man to win the Norris Trophy before Orr put an eight-year hammerlock on it, recalled that number 4's knees already showed the wear and tear that would prematurely end his career. Not that it mattered in the Cup finals.

"He'd limp around the arena, go out and get a few points, come off the ice and be limping again," Howell said in amazement.

Orr had four goals and four assists in Boston's six-game triumph, and his nineteen assists in the postseason bettered Beliveau's mark by three. There were thirty-three minors in the first two rough outings at Boston, where Ken Hodge had a Game One hat trick and a Game Two winner.

"Our power play did well in that series and Sanderson caused the Rangers' goalies [Ed Giacomin and Gilles Villemure] a lot of trouble," Bucyk said.

Orr's three-point effort in New York moved Boston up 3–1 in the series and he provided his second Cup-winning goal in a 3–0 Game Six shutout.

"Having won a Cup in our own building, the next best thing was winning one in New York," Bucyk said of the two cities' intense sports emotions.

Dryden and Esposito dueled again when the Habs and Hawks hooked up in 1973. A lot had gone under the bridge since 1971: both goalies had gone to war for Team Canada, Bowman replaced MacNeil and Hull departed Chicago. Fans settled down for what they thought would be a tight series.

"The newspapers played it up like a boxing match, the tale of the tape, Tony versus Ken," Dryden recalled.

Instead, they saw twenty-seven goals in the first three games. In Chicago's 8–7 win in Game Five, Dryden was beaten by the likes of Dave Kryskow and Len Frig.

Montreal lost a chance to take the Cup on home ice in Game Five and was down 2–0 early in Game Six. But Bowman's superior

Cheevers, with his famous mask showing where he'd been struck by pucks, helped the Bruins beat the New York Rangers for their second Cup in 1972.

The '72 finals were a hard-hitting affair.

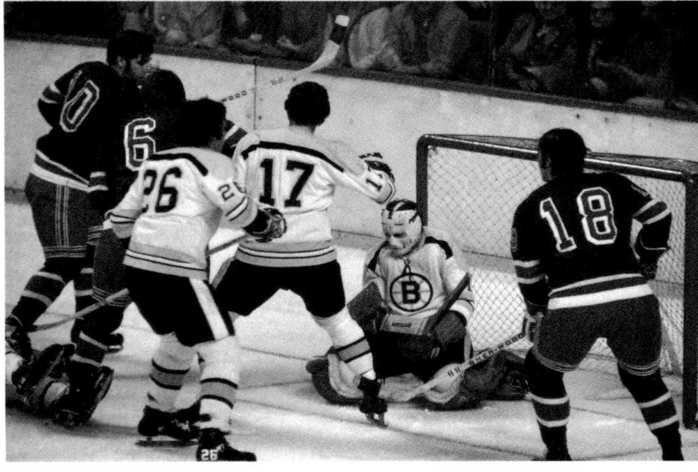

Boston goalie Ed Johnston makes a save in traffic.

The Bruins took great delight in winning the hard-fought series right in Madison Square Garden.

Chicago Black Hawks' Jim Pappin duels with Ken Dryden in a surprisingly high scoring 1973 final between the Hawks and the Canadiens.

The Bruins met their match in 1974 with the Broad Street Bullies from Philadelphia. Boston goalie Gilles Gilbert can't get a handle on an Orest Kindrachuk shot, as Wayne Cashman knocks Bill Barber to the ice.

bench won out. Cournoyer and Lemaire had twelve points each in the series, matching Gordie Howe's finals record. Richard retired a winner with his eleventh Cup and a gangly defenseman named Larry Robinson made a name for himself in the series.

"It was really something to win right in the Stadium, get the first Cup and to have a parade back home," Bowman said.

But it was the last time the Cup would be the exclusive property of the Original Six. The next club to lay claim would raise intimidation to an art form.

"Arrive first to the puck and in ill humor," late coach Fred "The Fog" Shero once advised his Philadelphia Flyers, a credo they still follow.

The Flyers had been building an abrasive team since the Blues beat them in early playoff meetings. Now they had Shero's ironclad system and a biker gang mentality to enter their first championship round.

The Spectrum had become a house of pain, yet the Flyers were underdogs to Boston, owing to the Bruins' home record of 17–0–2. So Flyers defenseman Joe Watson couldn't believe Shero's Game One pep talk.

"He told everyone that we had

"As (Bernie) Parent went, the team went," said Joe Watson of the Flyers. Parent allowed just three Spectrum goals in the 1974 finals against Boston.

already beaten a better team in the Rangers," Watson remembered. "I asked, 'Freddy, what the hell did you say that for?' He laughed and said, 'Reverse psychology.'"

The Flyers played the series hurt, minus Bob Kelly, while Gary Dornhoefer and Bill Clement were limited to three games each. Bruce Cowick was called up from Richmond and filled in admirably.

The script seemed to unfold as predicted, with four Flyer minors in the first period, leading to a Wayne Cashman power play goal. But Boston needed last-minute Orr heroics to win 3–2.

Philly's rogue element, such as Dave "Hammer" Schultz and Andre "Moose" Dupont, showed they could also score as the series progressed, joining Bobby Clarke in a three-goal rally to even the series.

"Dupont's goal [at 19:08 of Game Two] sent us on our way," Watson said. "Then Bernie Parent made an incredible save on Bucyk in overtime. That's when we knew for sure we had a chance."

Clarke netted the winner and Parent took control back on Broad Street, holding the Bruins to three goals in the three Spectrum games. Parent made thirty saves in a 2–0 deciding shutout, while Orr watched helplessly from the penalty box in the dying minutes. In seventeen playoff games, Parent was 12–5 with a goals against average of 2.02.

"Bernie was our salvation," Watson said of the Smythe winner. "As he went, the team went."

But the Flyers' success would almost be bettered by an even newer expansion team. The four-year-old Buffalo Sabres racked up 354 goals in 1974–75 and upset Montreal in the newly christened Wales Conference final.

"That spring, it was like all time had stopped in Buffalo," said forward Rick Dudley, now GM of the Tampa Bay Lightning. "You couldn't go anywhere without people recognizing you. They just adopted us and they would have gone berserk there if we'd won."

Two Flyer home victories did nothing to dampen spirits inside sweltering Memorial Auditorium in Buffalo. Fog patches developed on the ice, requiring the players to skate in circles to break up the soup. Rink personnel also donned blades and waved sheets to help.

No doubt attracted by the gloomy setting, a bat appeared in one game, dive-bombing the crowd, until it came in range of Sabre Jim Lorentz's stick.

"It was just above my head so I just whacked it," said Lorentz, now a team broadcaster. "I joked later that it was the only thing that Parent didn't stop in that series. Of course no one wanted to pick the darn thing up."

Rick MacLeish finally scooped it in his glove and took it to the

The Flyers' 1974 win over Boston was the first by an expansion team. Bobby Clarke (left) and Bernie Parent claim the trophy.

Graceful Gil Perreault and his Buffalo Sabres gave the Flyers a scare in 1975, but couldn't overcome Parent.

KOHO
SHER-WOOD

The Canadiens were geared to play the Flyers for the Cup from the moment the 1974–75 season began. Montreal's Ken Dryden and Jacques Lemaire look for the puck as Larry Robinson ties up Ross Lonsberry.

The Canadiens broke the Flyers' two-year hold on the Cup in 1976. Canadian Prime Minister Pierre Trudeau congratulates Serge Savard.

penalty box, despite Watson's warning it might be rabid. Lorentz was taken aback when he received some calls from irate bird lovers the next day.

"The funny thing was that when [Yankees outfielder] Dave Winfield killed that seagull in Toronto [in 1983], I was at that game," Lorentz said.

Amid the excitement, the Sabres won twice, including a Game Three overtime goal shared by "French Connection" stars Rene Robert, Gilbert Perreault and Rick Martin. The riled up Flyers allowed just one goal the rest of the way. Kelly broke a scoreless tie at the Aud early in the third and Parent's second Smythe was earned through fifty-five saves in Games Five and Six.

"Until I was a pro scout and saw Dominik Hasek play, I didn't think a goaltender could be that dominating," Dudley said of Parent.

Since Buffalo bounced them in the semifinals in 1975, the Canadiens were gearing for May of 1976 and what they perceived was an inevitable showdown with the Flyers.

"There was no way we were not going to beat them," Dryden declared. "Exhibition games against them counted in our mind and when we played a good team such as Chicago, we would imagine it was really Philadelphia."

Montreal advanced to the final handily, while the Flyers had to slog through a seven-game series with the Leafs and get past Boston. En route, they lost Parent for the season with an injury and turned to little-used backup Wayne Stephenson. MacLeish, a big playoff performer the past two years, was also absent.

With home ice, Bowman plotted several checking strategies to hound the Flyers top line of Clarke, Bill Barber and sniper Reggie Leach.

"Rather than put just one guy on Clarke, we put three; Lemaire, Doug Jarvis and Doug Risebrough," Bowman said. "Jacques had the offensive touch, Risebrough was aggressive and Jarvis was the great checker."

But perhaps the Canadiens were sharpened to too fine an edge.

"We were so geared for that first shift of Game One," Dryden said. "So what happens? Leach scores twenty-one seconds into the game."

Ross Lonsberry gave the Flyers a 2–0 margin, while Robinson

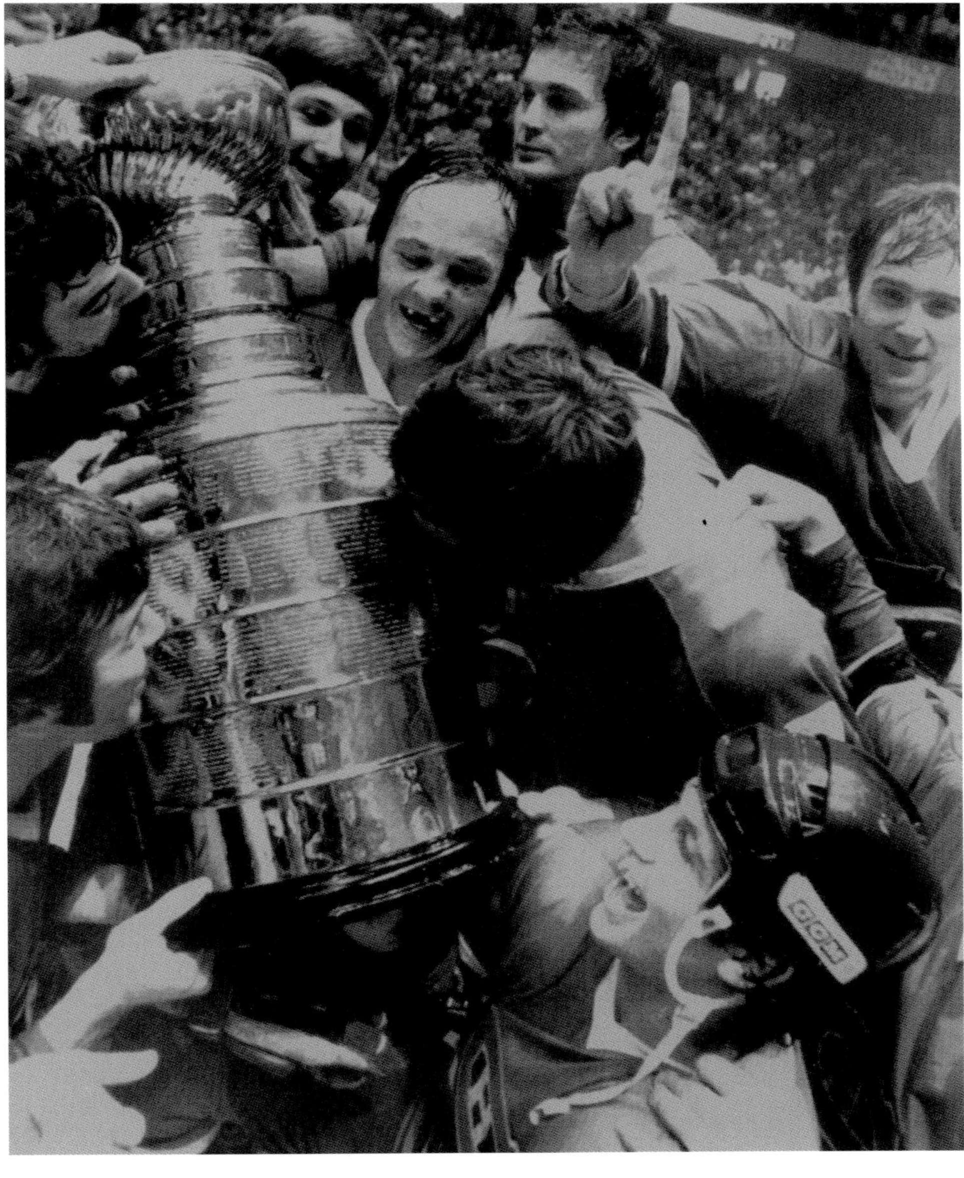

The last Montreal dynasty began in 1976 as they defeated the Flyers and began a string of four straight championships.

was on for two goals against. Collars tightened in the Forum, but not for long.

"My brother [Jimmy] had a chance to make it 3–0 and Dryden got that big shoulder on a puck," Joe Watson said sadly. "Otherwise it's 3–0, maybe they don't come back and the series changes dramatically."

However, thirty-six-year-old Roberts, nicknamed "Slow Boat to China," scored along with Robinson. Larry Goodenough gave the

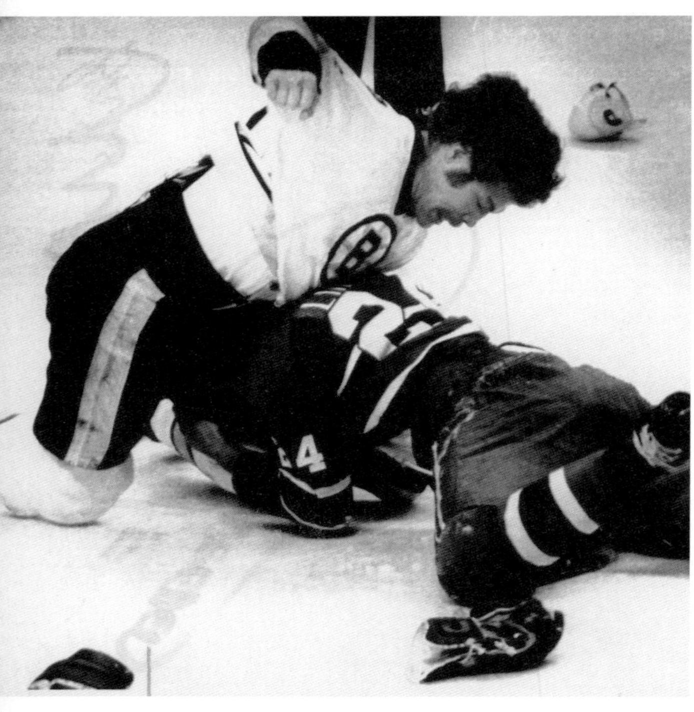

Montreal won two consecutive Cup finals from Boston in 1977 and 1978, but the Bruins' John Wensink goes down fighting in a scrap with Montreal's Gilles Lupien.

Flyers a 3–2 lead, before Lemaire and Guy Lapointe added third-period markers for a Montreal victory.

The talk of Game Two was a thundering hip check by Robinson on Dornhoefer that preceded a 2–1 win.

"They had to bring in hammers and crowbars to fix the dent in the boards," Dryden said. "It was a symbolic moment."

At the Spectrum, the Flyers turned to psychological warfare with Kate Smith. Whenever the aging "Songbird of the South" belted out "God Bless America," the Flyers had a near-perfect record. Watson agreed she was worth half a goal.

"All the talk to Game Three was 'Will Kate be there herself?'" Dryden said. "We'd never actually seen her, just the plaque in the building that showed her record. We kept saying there's no way she'll come. But in the warm-up, the red carpet comes out, the lights go down and there she is."

As the crowd went bonkers near the end of the song, the Habs broke from the blue line and began skating in a circle, faster and faster. They wanted to quiet the crowd quickly and did so with a Ric Chartraw hit on Joe Watson, then a Steve Shutt power play goal. Shutt scored again, after two Leach goals, and the 3–2 winner came from one of Montreal's policemen, Pierre Bouchard.

"That darn Bouchard got two goals in the playoffs against us and one the rest of the season," moaned Watson. "Most of the time against Montreal, it was like playing eight guys, they were so bloody fast. You wondered where the hell they were coming from."

Bouchard and Chartraw, who replaced Yvon Lambert after a groin injury, continued to give Montreal the physical edge in the latter part of the series. Meanwhile, Guy Lafleur, Shutt, Lemaire, Pete Mahovlich and the defense answered Leach's record nineteen goals. When Cournoyer, Lafleur and Mahovlich scored unanswered goals in a 5–3 clinching win, Dryden distributed the twenty-five copies of "God Bless America" he'd brought to Philly.

"We sang it all the way home," Dryden said. "[Forum anthem singer] Roger Doucet was on our flight and he changed the words to 'God Bless Our Canada.'" It wasn't long before Queen's period hit "We Are the Champions" would become the Habs' new anthem. Between 1976 and 1978, they lost just twenty-nine regular-season games and only six in the playoffs.

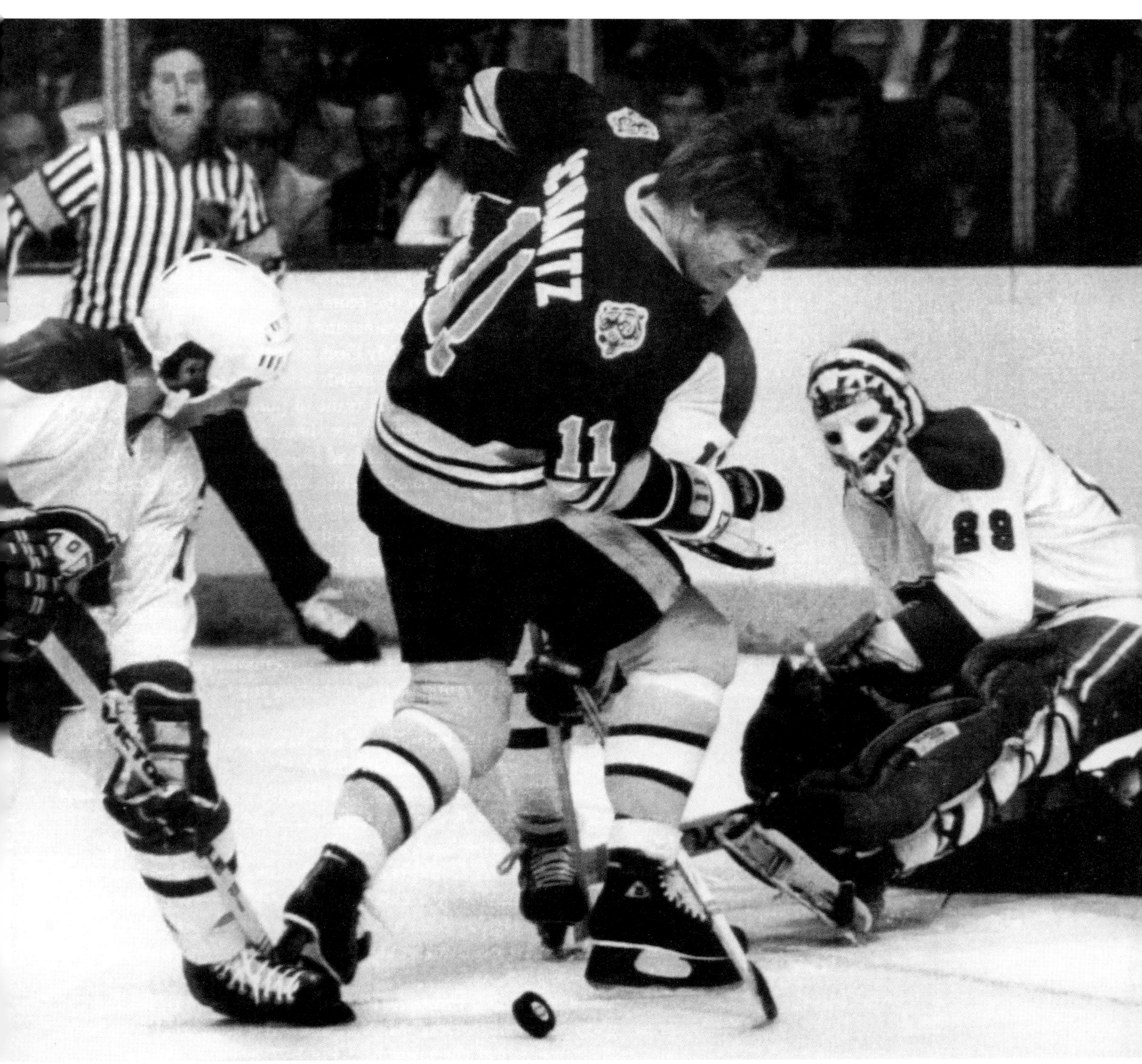

Dryden was a rock in goal for Montreal during the long Cup run. He watches Bobby Schmautz fight for the puck in front.

This might have been the only way to shut down Montreal snipers such as Steve Shutt. Shutt recovered from this spill to tie for the team high in goals in the 1978 final, with three.

Boston iced a Cup-caliber team in those days and were more physical, but they were still no match for Montreal in back-to-back finals in 1977 and 1978.

"When I'm in Montreal, I look at the pictures of those teams," Avalanche broadcaster and ex-Bruin Peter McNab said. "I think I saw nine Hall of Famers on the team we played, never mind Bowman and Pollock.

"My God, was that a fabulous team. Some nights you were out there thinking, 'I don't want to play against these guys, I want to get them all to sign my stick.'" Lafleur had five assists in the 1977 sweep, while wrapping up the Smythe with twenty-six playoff points.

"We tried everything to beat them that first year; practicing early, not practicing at all, coming to the rink early," McNab said. "Maybe we shouldn't have shown up at all." Blitzed 7–3 in the opener, Boston had just three goals the rest of the series. Lemaire picked up three of Montreal's game-winning goals, including the Cup winner in overtime.

The Bruins were less intimidated the next spring and both clubs needed just nine games to clash in the final.

"They won the first two games, but Cheesy [Gerry Cheevers] was unbelievable in Game Two when Lafleur scored in overtime," McNab said. "We came back to Boston and there was this huge ovation for him. [Gary Doak] scored in the first minute and we won 4–0. Suddenly, after losing six straight to them, we saw a light."

In Game Four, Gregg Sheppard scored in the opening minute and a Bobby Schmautz overtime goal past a screened Dryden won it in overtime 4–3.

"Now we're walking through [Boston's] Logan Airport, feeling pretty good about ourselves," McNab said. "But Montreal goes home and pulls a line out of the press box; Pierre Larouche, Pierre

Mondou and Mario Tremblay, three French Canadians, playing in the Forum. They're just zooming around—and these are their extra players." Habs defenseman Robinson and Boston's Brad Park led their respective teams in finals scoring, while Robinson's seventeen assists won him the Smythe.

Montreal's fourth trip to the finals began under a cloud but ended with their first Cup win on home ice since 1968.

"Going into the last game of the season, we needed a win against Detroit to pass the Islanders for first overall," Dryden said. "But we lost 1–0, an indication of things to come. We'd become a little sloppy, a little complacent."

Montreal was on the verge of losing their semifinal to the Bruins when coach Don Cherry was caught for too many men on the ice and the Habs pulled out two wins. The final opponent was the Rangers, who had the edge early with John Davidson outplaying Dryden in a Game One win.

"I had no idea where I'd left my game in that series," Dryden said of the 4–1 defeat. "This was a series with no guideposts for us. There I was, playing every minute of every playoff game since 1971 and Scotty pulls me in the third period.

"Bunny [Larocque] would probably play the rest of the way and I felt awful, knowing I'm going to retire after the series and wondering 'Is this the way it's going to end for me?'"

But a harmless looking Risebrough warm-up shot in Game Two struck Larocque's mask and Dryden had a chance at redemption. He and the Habs rolled to four straight victories.

"The last game in Montreal, the 4–1 night, was a perfect game," Bowman insisted. "I still have a tape of it that I get out and look at today. We were on the puck all the time."

Leading the way in the series was Smythe winner Bob Gainey. It was not just Dryden's last hurrah, as Bowman departed shortly after for the Sabres. Retirement also claimed Lemaire and Cournoyer.

"Everyone on that team felt they were in good hands; players with players, players with coaches, coaches with managers," Dryden said. "You couldn't point the finger and beg off responsibility. You didn't want to let anyone down. I would imagine it was the same feeling with the Islanders and their championships."

But the Islanders would have to forge their bonds the hard way.

OVELEAF: After a terrible start in the 1979 finals against the New York Rangers, Ken Dryden made saves like this one on Anders Hedberg to help the Canadiens get their confidence back.

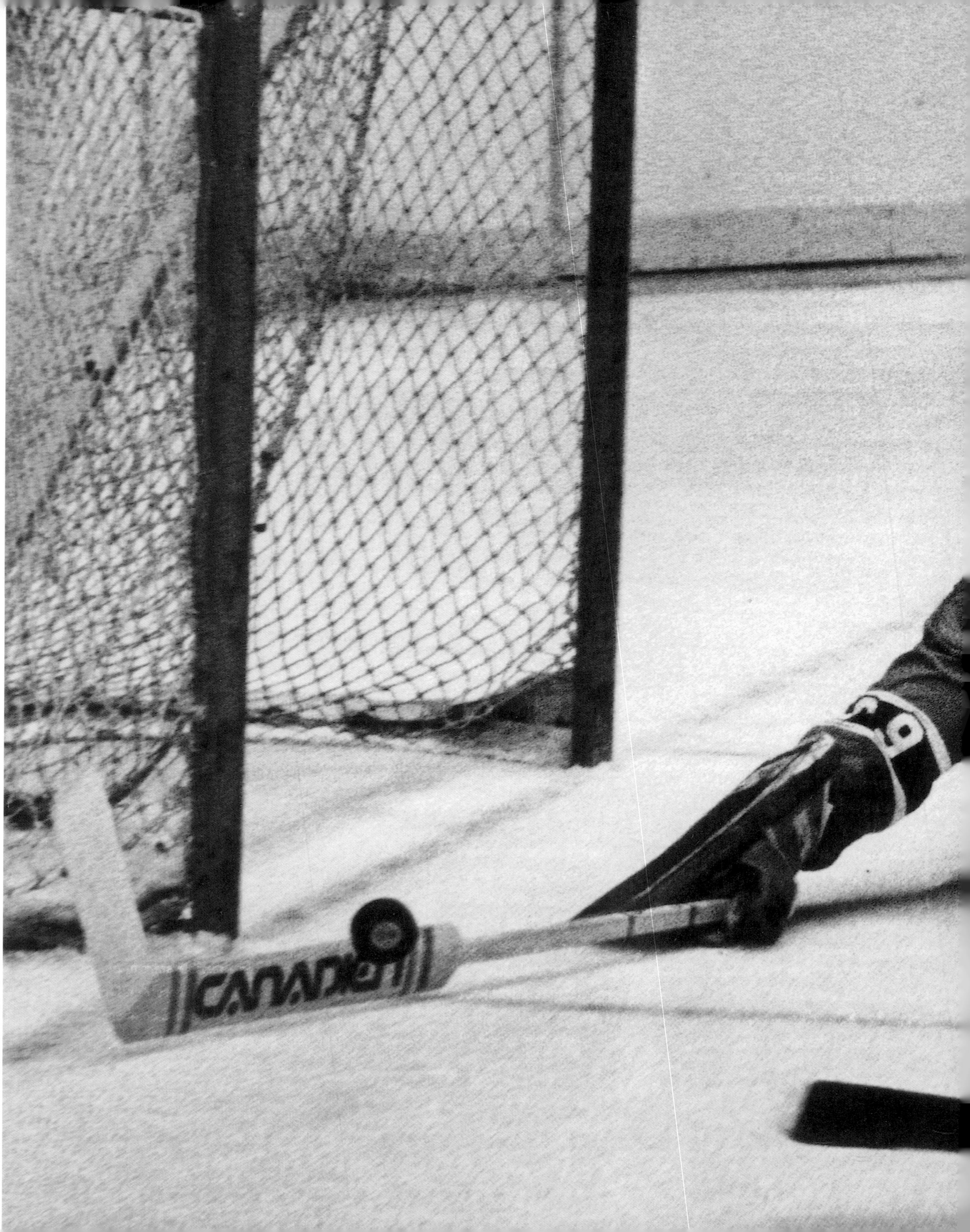

15

Conn Smythe winner Bob Gainey, who had five points and played outstanding two-way hockey, celebrates with the Cup after what Scotty Bowman called his team's "perfect game."

With a fourth consecutive Cup in the bag, Guy Lafleur leads Yvon Lambert, Doug Risebrough and Mario Tremblay over the boards to celebrate the five-game win over the Rangers.

From 1975 to 1979, the well-polished teams of general manager Bill Torrey and coach Arbour would hit a rut on the last turn to the championship series. Four times they lost in the semifinals, once in the quarters, two of their losses in seven-game series, one in overtime.

The Isles already boasted Mike Bossy and Bryan Trottier but retooled for 1979–80, retiring some veterans, adding role players and making low-key trades that turned into gold. In a late-season deal, Torrey added Butch Goring from L.A. and promoted Ken Morrow from the gold medal winning U.S. Olympic team.

Then came the playoffs, the first year all teams had to start with a best-of-five preliminary round. The Isles made it past L.A., Boston and Buffalo to play a no-name Flyers club that had still set a league-record thirty-five-game unbeaten streak.

The Flyers intended to restore their tough reputations by breaking New York's speed, skill and spirit in the Spectrum. A first-person magazine piece by Bossy that deplored fighting came out just before the series to encourage such sentiments on the Flyers' bench.

But in a Game One showdown with Mel Bridgman after a whistle, Bossy wouldn't skate around the Flyer's macho challenge, running right over him from twenty feet away. Denis Potvin's overtime goal, the first ever in Cup history on the power play, allowed the Isles to split at the Spectrum and go on to a 3–2 series lead.

"It was a very physical series," Pat Quinn said of coaching the Flyers. "We beat the Islanders five on five, but they killed us on the power play.

"There had been troubles with their team a little earlier that year and fans were calling for Arbour to be replaced. Luckily management didn't see the wisdom in that. Much like Detroit or New Jersey in the 1990s, the Islanders had to learn how to win."

Game Six was war in Uniondale, a 2–2 first-period tie marred by sixteen penalties. Bossy and Bob Nystrom scored for New York in the second, the latter's goal clearly offside to everyone but the linesman. Bob Dailey and John Paddock struck for Philly in the third.

"We were down in the dumps because we'd been up two goals," Nystrom said. "But we had a saying going into overtime to whip it up in the room—'Who will be the hero tonight?'"

There would be a few of them in the 7:11 it took to win. Billy

OVERLEAF: No one expected to see the Minnesota North Stars in the finals against the mighty New York Islanders in 1981, but here, Dino Ciccarelli gave Billy Smith a hard time here as Denis Potvin closes in.

23
AINEY

The Islanders were blessed with a strong defensive component, as Bryan Trottier shows his shot-blocking abilities to Flyers' Behn Wilson.

The Flyers hoped to manhandle the upstart Isles in their first taste of Cup finals action in 1980. But Bob Bourne shows he can stand up to Norm Barnes in the series.

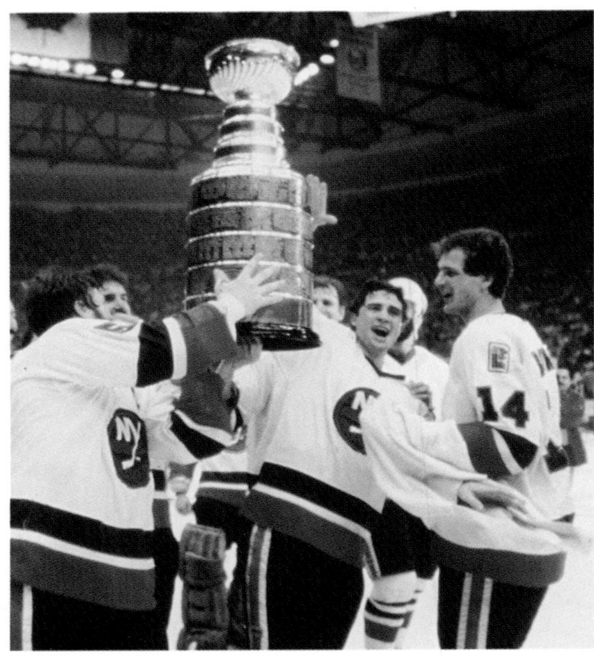

After many heartbreaking losses trying to reach the Cup finals, the Islanders made the most of their first trip in 1980 and beat the Flyers in six games.

Smith stopped Clarke, and then John Tonelli and Nystrom broke away two-on-one on Dailey.

"We'd worked that play in practice many times, trying to get the defenseman to come up," Nystrom said. "Dailey bit on it and I was able to get it in."

Tonelli's quick pass left Nystrom with just one option—extend his blade and tip the puck, a move that fooled Pete Peeters. It was his fourth overtime goal of the playoffs and the Islanders were champions.

"Until that moment, we were considered a team of losers and chokers," Arbour said. "If Nystrom doesn't score who knows what happens to our team?"

With a lineup virtually unchanged, the Islanders added nineteen points and emerged in first place overall for the 1980–81 regular season. In the playoffs, they lost just two games to the upstart Edmonton Oilers in the quarterfinals before reaching the championship.

New York opened their defense of the crown against a Minnesota team that had won a seven-game series against the Flyers and beaten the high-scoring Calgary Flames in six.

"That Minnesota team surprised a lot of people," Nystrom said. "Dino Ciccarelli was a real fan favorite and they had an incredible power play; Steve Payne on left wing, Dino on right, Bobby Smith in the middle. Their building was really big on fan involvement. It was a tough place to play."

Ciccarelli's twenty-one overall playoff points would break Don Maloney's rookie record, but another huge series by Bossy, joined by Wayne Merrick (eight points each) and Goring (seven points) sealed a five-game victory.

Bossy, who ended up with thirty-five playoff points after fifty goals in fifty regular-season games, was upset at being beaten out for the Smythe by Goring. The latter had a Game Three hat trick and the winning goal in a 7–5 result at the Met Center, a crushing blow to the Stars at home.

Arbour, who had once played for Bowman in St. Louis, was as demanding as the latter during the Isles' rise to power but was more of a players' coach.

"I wouldn't call myself loose," Arbour said. "But my job was easier

The Vancouver Canucks pulled a few upsets along the road to the 1982 finals, but ran up against Battlin' Billy Smith and the seasoned Islanders in the final.

31
19
LANGEVIN
26

In this one-sided board meeting, the Isles' Bryan Trottier sends a Canuck tumbling over the boards in the 1982 finals.

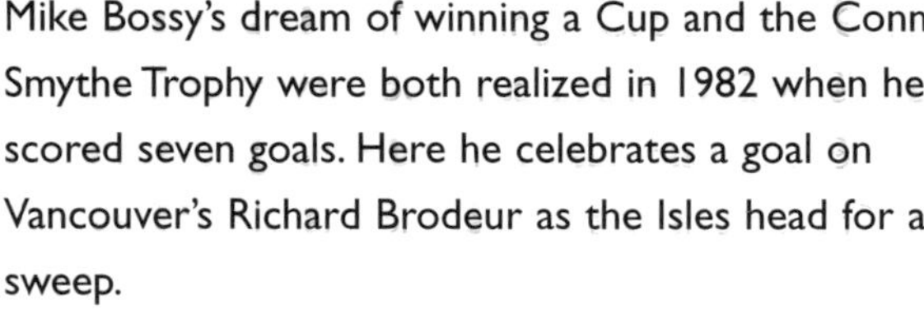

Mike Bossy's dream of winning a Cup and the Conn Smythe Trophy were both realized in 1982 when he scored seven goals. Here he celebrates a goal on Vancouver's Richard Brodeur as the Isles head for a sweep.

Goaltender Billy Smith taunted the frustrated Edmonton Oilers throughout their first trip to the Cup finals. Here, he blocks Jari Kurri as Butch Goring tries to help.

because there was a lot of accountability on that team. No one went babbling to the press with complaints, it all stayed in the room.

"The veterans—Trottier, Gillies, Potvin, Tonelli—they all made sure new guys adhered. You had a team that didn't rely on just one or two guys." The balanced attack produced a third trip to the finals in 1982, against the Vancouver Canucks.

On paper, the Canucks shouldn't have been there—three games below .500 in the regular season with a relative popgun offense. Coach Harry Neale had been suspended by the league in a regular-season incident and Roger Neilson was at the helm.

"We were like many playoff teams I've seen before and since; with players who suddenly play the best hockey of their careers for the two months of playoffs," Neale said. "Thomas Gradin, Stan Smyl and Curt Fraser was a good line for us. But we were missing a lot of guys with injuries.

"We had brought in guys such as Neil Belland, who played as good or better than the guy he'd replaced. I'm sure the Islanders at first wondered, 'Who are these guys?'

"But the Islanders were like the Oilers later on. They could beat you in many different ways."

The Canucks had home-ice advantage right up until the finals because of upsets in other series. But the Isles triumphed in Uniondale, starting 6–5 in overtime.

"Harold Snepsts had a pass picked off [by Mike Bossy] with two seconds to go in the overtime period," Neale said ruefully. "We were pretty good in the second game [until eleven Isles had a point in a four-goal third period] and that was a close as we came. We found out how far we could come, but how far we still had to go."

Predictably, Canucks' ruffian Dave "Tiger" Williams attempted to rattle the Isles both verbally and physically.

"They had Williams on Bossy all the time, but Bossy was unstoppable," Nystrom said. "He even scored one in midair."

That amazing marker came in Game Three at the PNE Coliseum, on the follow-through of a rebound from in tight on Richard Brodeur. Lars Lindgren of the Canucks tripped Bossy, but Brodeur's second save came back as Bossy was airborne. With only his blade touching the ice, he got off a backhand that beat both the goalie and sliding defenseman Colin Campbell.

Bossy had three of the team's six goals in the two Vancouver games, completing the sweep. This time Bossy received the Smythe as his seven goals tied the 1956 finals record of Beliveau, two of the goals coming on the power play in Game Four. Trottier's thirty-two assists were a playoff record, and Smith broke his own wins record in that 3–1 finale, raising his playoff record to 15–4.

"That was the first time we won the Cup on the road and it had to be the greatest party of the four," Nystrom said. "The Cup was on board the plane ride home and for four hours there was no one but us, a chance to be together. It was the greatest feeling in the world."

It was also the first time a U.S.-based team had won three straight titles, but as Bossy observed in his book: "I knew our reign was about to be challenged. I knew we were going to see Edmonton soon."

The young, cocky Oilers had caught the attention of the Isles two years earlier when they were singing on the bench during a six-game quarterfinal.

OVERLEAF: Conn Smythe Trophy winner Billy Smith would do anything to win, whether it was in the rule book or not. He became the fourth different Isle to win the playoff MVP award. He saved his worst treatment for Gretzky as seen in one of their encounters in 1983

Wayne Gretzky (left) and the young Oilers had to absorb some hard lessons from Bryan Trottier and the Islanders in their Cup meeting in 1983.

KOHO
31

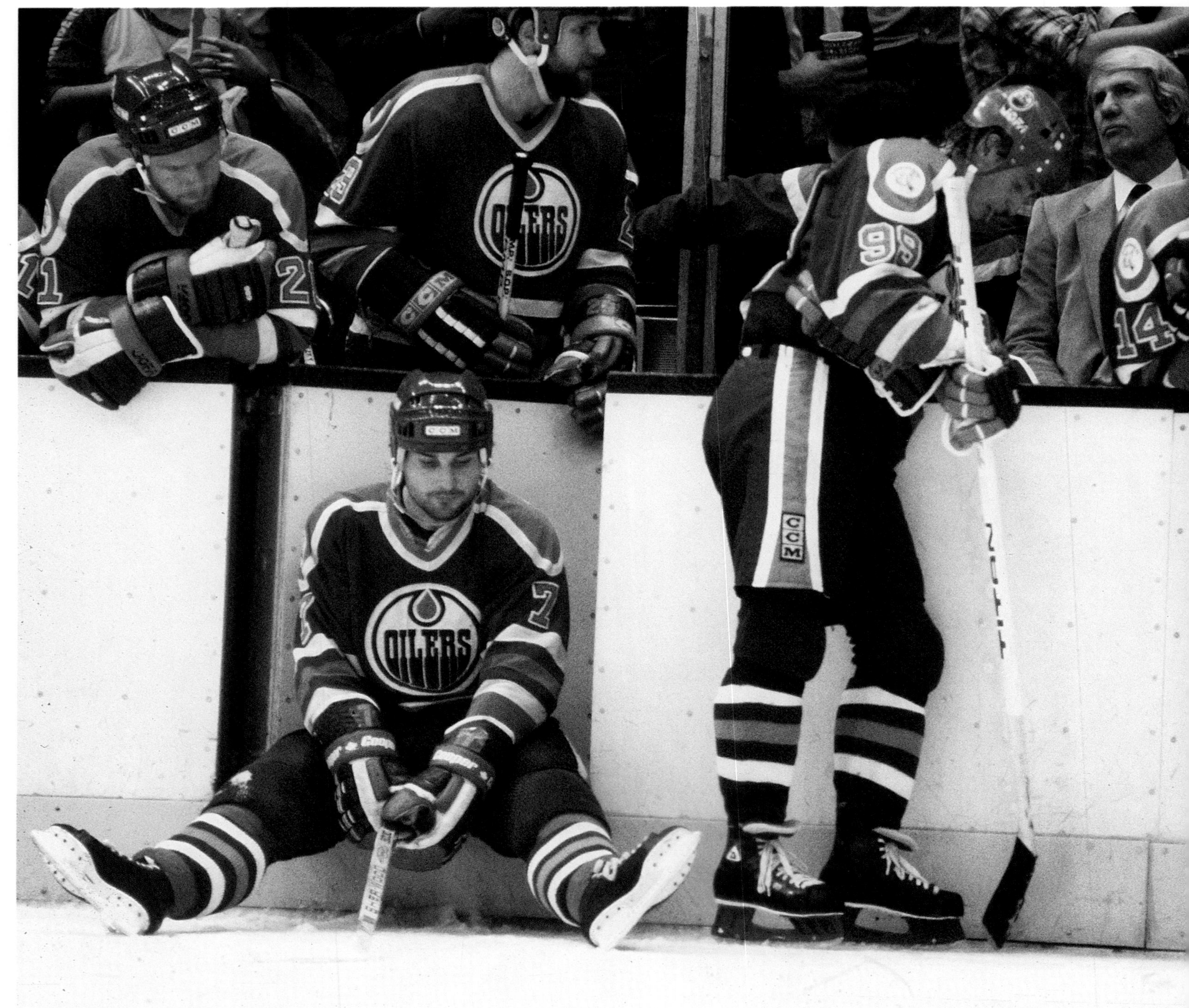
OILERS
OILERS
CCM

Paul Coffey slumps in the doorway of the Oilers' bench with a dejected Wayne Gretzky nearby as the Islanders celebrate a win in the 1983 finals. The Oilers' time would come.

The Oilers could obviously score, with 424 goals in the regular season and routs of Calgary and Chicago leading to their first finals appearance in 1983. Bossy was a Game One scratch with food poisoning. But the Oilers had much to learn about winning in May as New York systematically wore them down.

"They took more punishment than we did," Gretzky said in his autobiography. "They dove into more boards and stuck their faces into more pucks."

The Isles also had the nefarious Smith, who unnerved Edmonton forwards every time they crossed the blue line.

"If any money was on the line, you wanted Smitty," Arbour said. "He'd chop and slash to make a point."

He would allow only six goals in another sweep, though Game One was up in the air until a Morrow empty-net goal.

"We knew Gretz, Paul Coffey and Mark Messier were a force, but our win was a real tribute to our system," Nystrom said. "We hit Gretzky and we bothered Anderson."

Smith had himself assailed as public enemy number one in Edmonton when he slashed Gretzky in Game Two and took great delight in telling the media how he faked an injury from an Anderson slash that cost the Oilers a penalty in a tight Game Four. He was also the Smythe winner, underlining the club's depth by becoming the fourth different Isle of the dynasty to be named.

"People said [1983] would be the end of the line for us, so it was very satisfying to win it again," Morrow said.

"The thing that catapulted us to those Cups was great character," Nystrom added. "If you met any one of those guys on the street today, you would still see they have it."

Offense Ascendant—Defense Resurgent 1984–2000

Throughout the eighties Wayne Gretzky would shatter scoring records by such margins as to redefine what was humanly possible, and he would do so while leading the Edmonton Oilers to a dynastic four Stanley Cups.

As the twentieth century moved toward its close, Wayne Gretzky was becoming the most statistically dominant athlete ever in the history of North American team sports, not merely breaking records by small increments but shattering them by such margins as to redefine what was humanly possible. By the mid-1980s, Gretzky and his Edmonton Oiler teammates had ushered in a new era of wide-open hockey that did not end until it was strangled by the sophisticated defenses and dominant goaltenders of the 1990s. But even a team as gifted as the Oilers had to learn the hard way that setting records is one thing, winning the Stanley Cup is something much tougher.

Late on the night of May 17, 1983, Gretzky and Kevin Lowe of the Edmonton Oilers slunk past the Nassau Coliseum dressing room of the New York Islanders, the team that had just broomed Edmonton out of the playoffs in four straight while clinching a fourth consecutive Stanley Cup. Gretzky and Lowe expected to be bitter witnesses to the sights and sounds of jubilation in the New York dressing room. What they saw instead was Islander center Bryan Trottier icing a bruised knee, defenseman Denis Potvin getting treated for a dislocated shoulder and other battered Islanders limping around with black eyes and stitched cuts.

After looking at the Islanders, Gretzky turned to Lowe and said, "That's why they won and we lost." In his autobiography, *Gretzky*, the game's greatest scorer recalled of that series: "They sacrificed everything they had."

"That," said Lowe to Gretzky, "is how you win championships."

A year later, in possibly the most consequential Stanley Cup final ever, the dynastic Islanders' "Drive for Five" met the high-scoring Oilers' "Gun for One." It would be a test of New York's old-fashioned North American muck-and-grind linear orthodoxy against the dazzling up-tempo Euro-swirl of the Oilers. But by 1984, the

Edmonton super-pest Ken Linseman crashes the Islander cage in the 1984 finals as New York goalie Battlin' Billy Smith ties up the puck and defenseman Stefan Persson looks on. This was the year the Oilers added grit to their stylish game and wrested the Cup from the four-time champion Islanders.

OVERLEAF: Edmonton goaltender Grant Fuhr—who teammate Wayne Gretzky had called "the best goalie in the world"—makes a split save on Islander forward Greg Gilbert in the 1984 finals. Fuhr's playoff stats were eleven wins, four losses, 2.99 GAA and .910 save percentage.

OILERS
VIC

TONELLI

Islander captain Denis Potvin (left) and Oiler center Mark Messier joust in the 1984 finals. Messier's eight goals, twenty-six points and "follow-me-boys" leadership throughout the playoffs would win him the Conn Smythe Trophy as playoff MVP.

maturing Oilers had added some grit to their stylish game.

In Game One in New York, Kevin McClelland—an Oiler better known for his fists than his hands—supplied a goal and Grant Fuhr picked up a shutout as the Oilers gutted out an ugly 1–0 win that sent a message: we can play it any way you want to play it. But Gretzky, who was goalless in the 1983 finals, was now pointless and by Game Two it looked as though the Isles suffocating defense could choke off the Oilers' best-in-the-league offense. New York won a 6–1 blowout, Gretzky again had neither a goal nor an assist, and under the 2–3–2 format of the time, the teams headed for three games in Edmonton—three games that would change the face of hockey for a decade.

The Oilers won Game Three in a 7–2 blitz, though Gretzky would be held scoreless for the third time in the series, the seventh consecutive time in the finals and the tenth consecutive time versus the Islanders. It was then that assistant coach John Muckler took Gretzky aside and said, "Don't worry about scoring so many goals. But when you get one make it a big one." Gretzky did. In the first

OVERLEAF: Edmonton forward Kent Nilsson (15) and Philadelphia goalie Ron Hextall became the focal points of the 1987 finals following Hextall's chop to the back of Nilsson's knees in Game Four. Hextall would be suspended for eight games, but not until the next season.

The Oilers 1984 Cup win represented the triumph of an up-tempo, Euro-swirl style over linear bump-and-grind orthodoxy epitomized above by the New York Islanders tough-checking winger John Tonelli.

27
VIC

D.SMITH

Edmonton right wing Jari Kurri splits the Philly defense—including Mark Howe (2)—in a race for the puck in the 1985 finals, which were won by the Oilers four games to one. Kurri had nineteen goals in eighteen playoff games and his four hat tricks (including one four-goal game) broke Mark Messier's record of three.

period of Game Four, Gretzky took a pass from bodyguard Dave Semenko, deked New York goalie Billy Smith and put a backhander upstairs for the first of his two goals in another 7–2 rout.

The day before Game Five, Walden's, an upscale Edmonton restaurant, was offering roast Long Island Duckling as its specialty of the day. The smell of Islander blood seemed to waft throughout the city. Gretzky sensed more than blood. In the Oiler dressing room, minutes before the players filed out for the opening faceoff, Gretzky stood up and told his teammates: "I've won a lot of awards in my life. I've had a lot of personal success. But nothing I've ever done means more than this."

Gretzky carried that leadership onto the ice with two first-period goals, both on perfect passes from linemate Jari Kurri. With Mark Messier hammering Islanders in the corners and with defenseman Paul Coffey performing like a one-man breakout play, the Oilers skated to a 5–2 Cup-clinching win, ending one dynasty and launching another. Starting in 1984, Edmonton would win five of the next seven Stanley Cups and begin a streak in which Canadian teams would win seven Cups in a row. But, in the champagne mist and rollicking chaos of the Edmonton dressing room minutes after the Islanders' elimination, it was Gretzky who captured the significance of his team's win: "I hope we're an influence on the game. We proved that an offensive team can win the Cup. And that can't do anything but help hockey."

But the next season Gretzky and his teammates had to learn a fundamental truth about the Stanley Cup. "The Cup is addictive," wrote Gretzky in his autobiography. "You think it's yours and so you become like a selfish kid—you don't want anybody else to touch it, see it, have it or study it." In 1985, the Philadelphia Flyers wanted to do all of those things. This was the Flyer team of ninety-eight-point scorer Tim Kerr, legendary defenseman Mark Howe and hard-driving and inscrutable coach Mike Keenan. The Oilers destroyed them in one of the greatest offensive explosions in Cup history.

After dropping a lackluster 4–1 game on the choppy ice of the Philadelphia Spectrum—a game so bad that Oilers coach Glen Sather burned the videotapes—the Oilers gushed goals, running the table 3–1, 4–3, 5–3 and a final-game-record 8–3. Gretzky's seven goals in the five games tied a record held by Jean Beliveau (1956) and Mike Bossy (1982). Kurri had nineteen goals in eighteen playoff games to tie the record for goals in one playoff year, and his four hat tricks (including one four-goal game) broke Messier's record of three. Coffey's twelve goals, twenty-five assists and thirty-seven points shattered Bobby Orr's record for playoff goals (nine) and assists (nineteen), and Denis Potvin's record for points (twenty-five). "All I know," said Gretzky after that series, "is that someday I'm going to say, 'Geez, I played on a great team.'"

Said Coffey: "We haven't won four or five in a row yet. But this might be a start of a dynasty."

It would be a dynasty interrupted by a train wreck.

Oiler Mark Messier runs into Flyer defenseman Miroslav Dvorak during goal-mouth action in the 1985 finals in which Edmonton would outscore the Flyers 21–14, including an 8–3 thrashing in the fifth and deciding game.

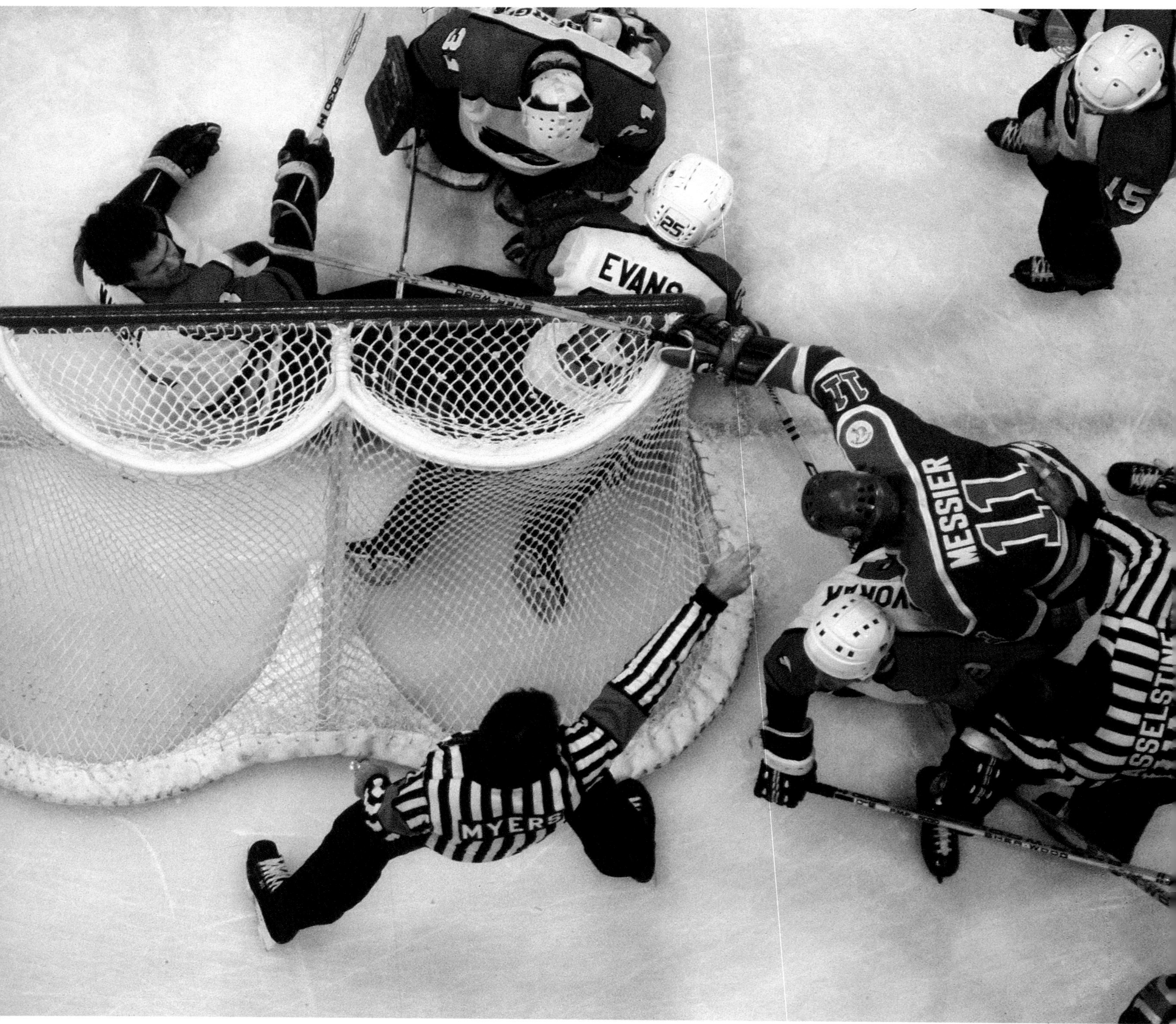

Mark Messier runs over the Flyers' Ron Sutter in 1985. Messier had two goals and six assists, for eight points in a deciding round in which the Oilers gushed goals and began to take on the aura of a dynasty.

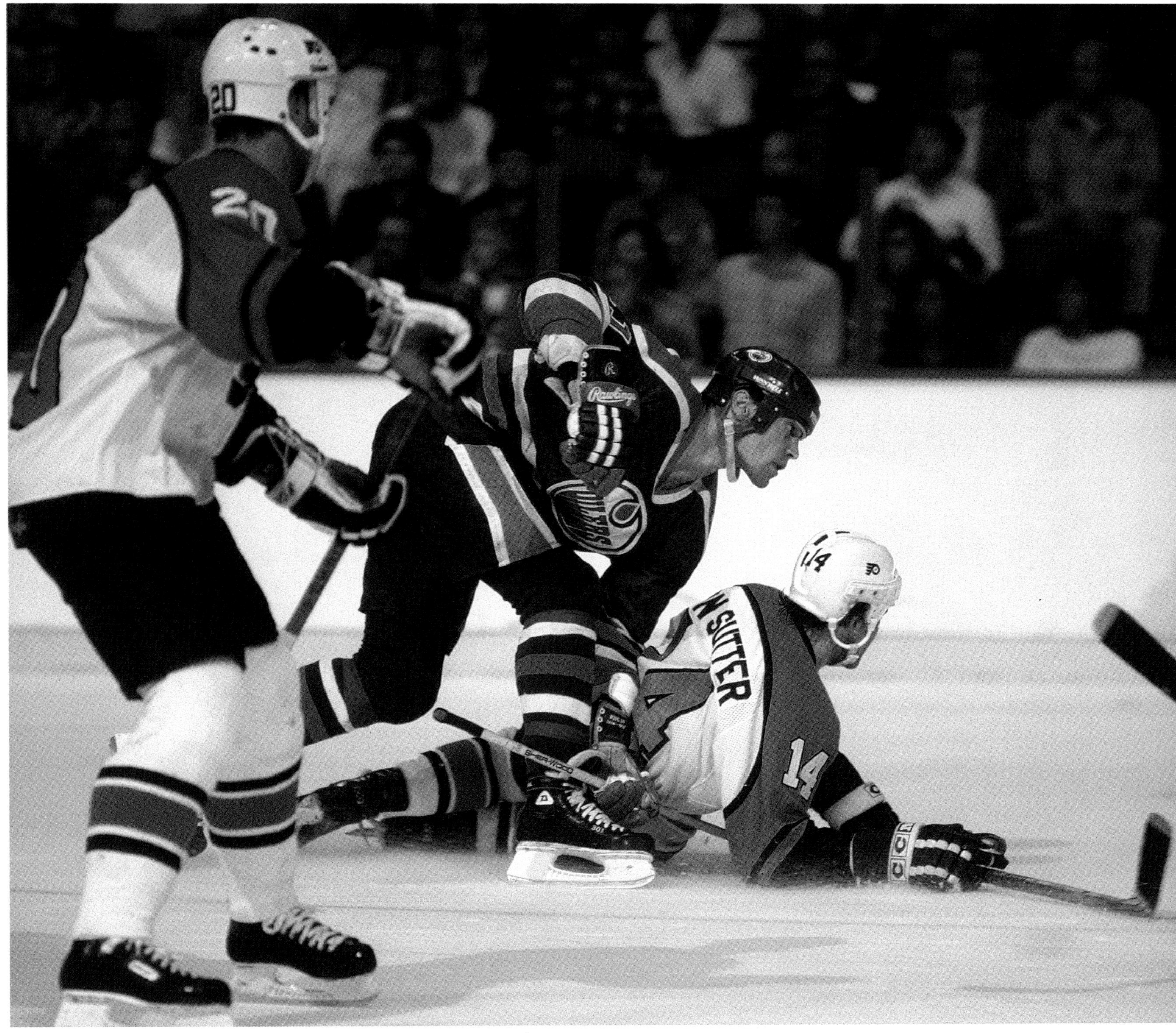

After a regular season in which the Oilers finished with 119 points—nine ahead of the Flyers in the overall standings—and Gretzky set a league record for assists (163) and points (215), the young, cocky Oilers looked like a team that could take a run at Montreal's NHL record of five consecutive Stanley Cups. But, after crushing Vancouver by a combined score of 17–3 in a sweep of the best-of-five first round, Edmonton met arch rival Calgary in another "Battle of Alberta." The teams split the first six games and then the surprising Flames took a 2–0 lead in the second period of Game Seven. No sweat. No panic. The Oilers tied it up before the end of the period and went to the dressing room collectively thinking, as Gretzky recalled, "We're all right. Let's freeze them out, get us a goal and go suck some beers." But late in the third period, Edmonton defenseman Steve Smith took control of Perry Berezan's dump-in off to the left of the Oilers' goal and tried to make a cross-ice pass in front of his own net. The puck hit the side of Edmonton goalie Grant Fuhr's left leg and caromed into the net. Berezan was credited with the goal. After the play, Smith skated to the bench, sat down and broke into tears. "[It was] a horrible, unlucky, incredible accident," said Gretzky. The Oilers lost 3–2 and the Flames went on to meet Montreal in a final made memorable by Les Canadiens' twenty-year-old rookie goalie, Patrick Roy. After splitting games in Calgary, the teams returned to the Montreal Forum where the storied "Cathedral of Hockey" would soon be colloquially renamed St. Patrick's Cathedral. Montreal took a 5–3 win in Game Three and then watched Roy pitch the first shutout by a rookie in a Stanley Cup final in twenty-nine years as he led *Nos Glorieux* to within a game of the Cup.

Back in Calgary, the Habs were up 4–3 with fourteen seconds to play when Roy made an incredible toe save on a Jamie Macoun shot to seal the Canadiens' record twenty-third Stanley Cup. Roy's fifteen playoff wins and 1.92 average made him the youngest player to win the Conn Smythe Trophy.

The 1987 playoffs produced the NHL's first seven-game final in sixteen seasons, a rematch of the 1985 Oilers-Flyers final, only this time in a series marked by drama, marred by controversy and interspersed with humor.

Edmonton won the first two games 4–2 and 3–2 (the latter in

Edmonton goalie Grant Fuhr butterflies to stop Philadelphia's Lindsay Carson in the 1987 finals, won by the Oilers. This was the year in which Fuhr, explaining to writers why he'd played eighteen holes of golf before Game Five said, "Because there wasn't enough daylight to play thirty-six."

overtime), but following Game Two Philly coach Mike Keenan accused Gretzky of "diving" to draw penalties. "You expect more from the best hockey player in the world," said Keenan. When Gretzky went down from a Lindsay Carson trip in front of the Philly bench, Keenan yelled, "Earn your chances!"

The teams split the next two games in Philadelphia (5–3 Flyers, 4–1 Oilers). As the series shifted back to Edmonton, the media continued to play up Keenan's "diving" charges and the Oilers' counterattack, wherein they complained long and loud about Philly goalie Ron Hextall's chop on the back of Kent Nilsson's knees (for which Hextall would be suspended for eight games but not until the next season). It was here that Edmonton goalie Grant Fuhr provided one of the better bits of comic relief in Stanley Cup lore. On the off-day before Game Five, Fuhr played eighteen holes of golf. Asked by a reporter how a goalie could play eighteen holes during a Stanley Cup final, the unflappable Fuhr said, "There wasn't enough daylight to play thirty-six."

Hextall's goaltending led Philadelphia to two wins to even the series, force Game Seven in Edmonton and clinch the Conn Smythe Trophy for the Flyer's goalie. But when Edmonton won its third Cup in four years, with a 3–1 victory, it was Gretzky who made hockey's most historic and moving trophy presentation. After raising the Cup over his head, Gretzky passed it directly to defenseman Steve Smith, the goat of the 1986 playoffs. Said Smith: "I was in tears last year, and I'm in tears this year. But this year they're tears of joy."

There wasn't much doubt that the Edmonton Oilers would win the 1988 Stanley Cup by beating a plucky but out-gunned Boston Bruins team that

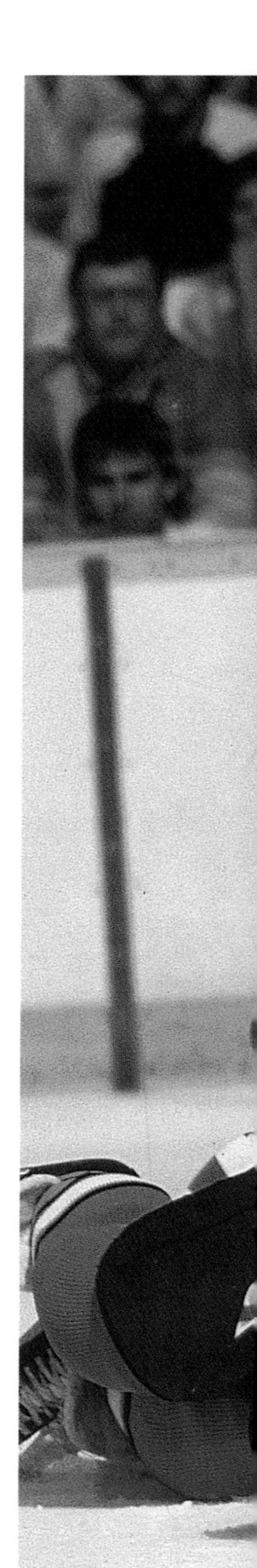

Edmonton's Mark Messier hammers Philadelphia's Peter Zezel to the ice as Paul Coffey (7) looks on. The 1987 finals—won by the Oilers—was the first final series in sixteen years to go seven games.

CCM
WINN WELL
OILERS
Rawlings
P. 9030
7030 FEATHER-GLAS SHER-WOOD

was making its first appearance in a Cup final in ten years. But no one expected hockey's first and only "five-game sweep." After the Oilers won the first two games in Edmonton, the series moved to ancient and unair-conditioned Boston Garden, which, in the heat of late May, was New England's biggest steam bath. The Oilers hammered the Bruins 6–3 in Game Three and looked like a lock to win the Stanley Cup on the road, something they'd never done.

With the Bruins leading 3–2 with 3:23 left in the second period, Edmonton's Craig Simpson tied the score. But public address man Joel Permutter's announcement of Simpson's goal was abruptly cut off when a 4,000-volt electrical switch blew out and the Garden was plunged into darkness. "They had just enough electricity in this old barn to flip the red light on, and that was it," said Oiler scout Ace Bailey, an ex-Bruin.

According to league bylaws, the game was suspended and would be made up in its entirety only if the series went seven games. It didn't. The series went back to Edmonton where the Oilers took an easy 6–3 win for their fourth Cup in five years, a dynasty by all but the most conservative definitions. Gretzky's Cup final series record of thirteen points (three goals, ten assists versus Boston and an astonishing twelve goals, thirty-one assists, forty-three points for the playoffs) earned him the Conn Smythe Trophy and the praise of Bruins coach Terry O'Reilly. "There should be a rule that [Gretzky] has to get passed around from team to team every year," said O'Reilly in an observation that would prove disquietingly prophetic. Less than three months later, on August 9, Wayne Gretzky and teammates Marty McSorley and Mike Krushelnyski were traded to the L.A. Kings for Jimmy Carson, Martin Gelinas, three first-round draft picks and—the biggest reason for the biggest trade in hockey history—U.S.$15 million, which went to the Oilers' cash-strapped owner Peter Pocklington.

Gretzky's trade and the resultant weakening of the Oilers left the door ajar for Edmonton's arch provincial rivals, the Calgary Flames, heretofore perennial runners-up in the "Battle of Alberta." After finishing fifth overall, the Flames rode the goaltending of Mike Vernon (a record-tying sixteen playoff wins) and the play of defenseman Al MacInnis (the leading playoff scorer with seven goals, twenty-four assists, thirty-one points) to their first-ever

Wayne Gretzky is stopped by Flyer goaltender Ron Hextall in 1987, the year in which Hextall played so well he joined goalies Roger Crozier of the '66 Red Wings and Glenn Hall of the '68 Blues, and forward Reggie Leach of the '76 Flyers as the only players on a losing club to earn the Conn Smythe Trophy.

OVERLEAF: The ancient, unair-conditioned and now demolished Boston Garden was New England's biggest steam bath when, in the late-May heat of 1988, the Oilers and the Bruins met in a final that turned into a five-game sweep for Edmonton.

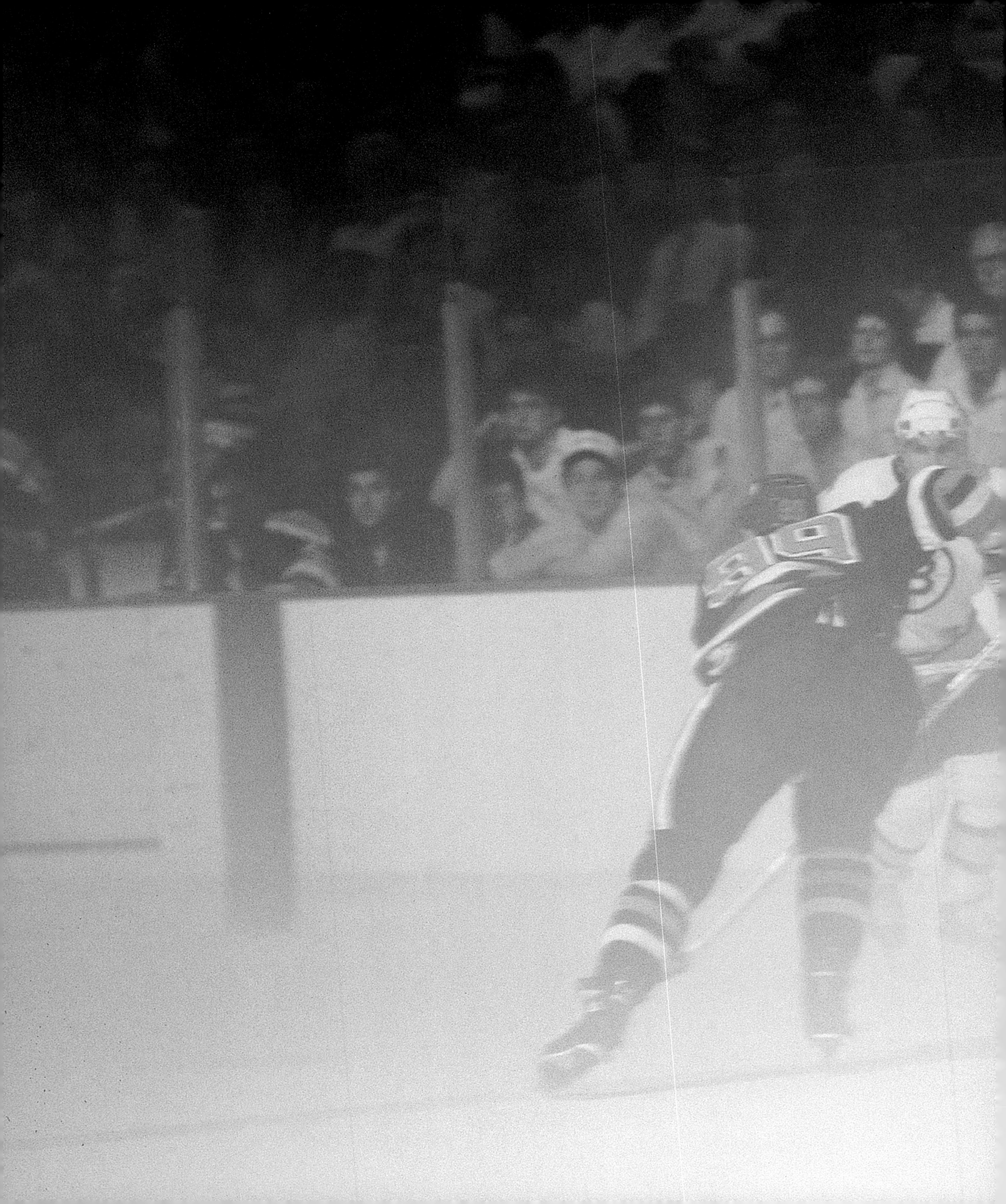

MESSIER
11
NIKE

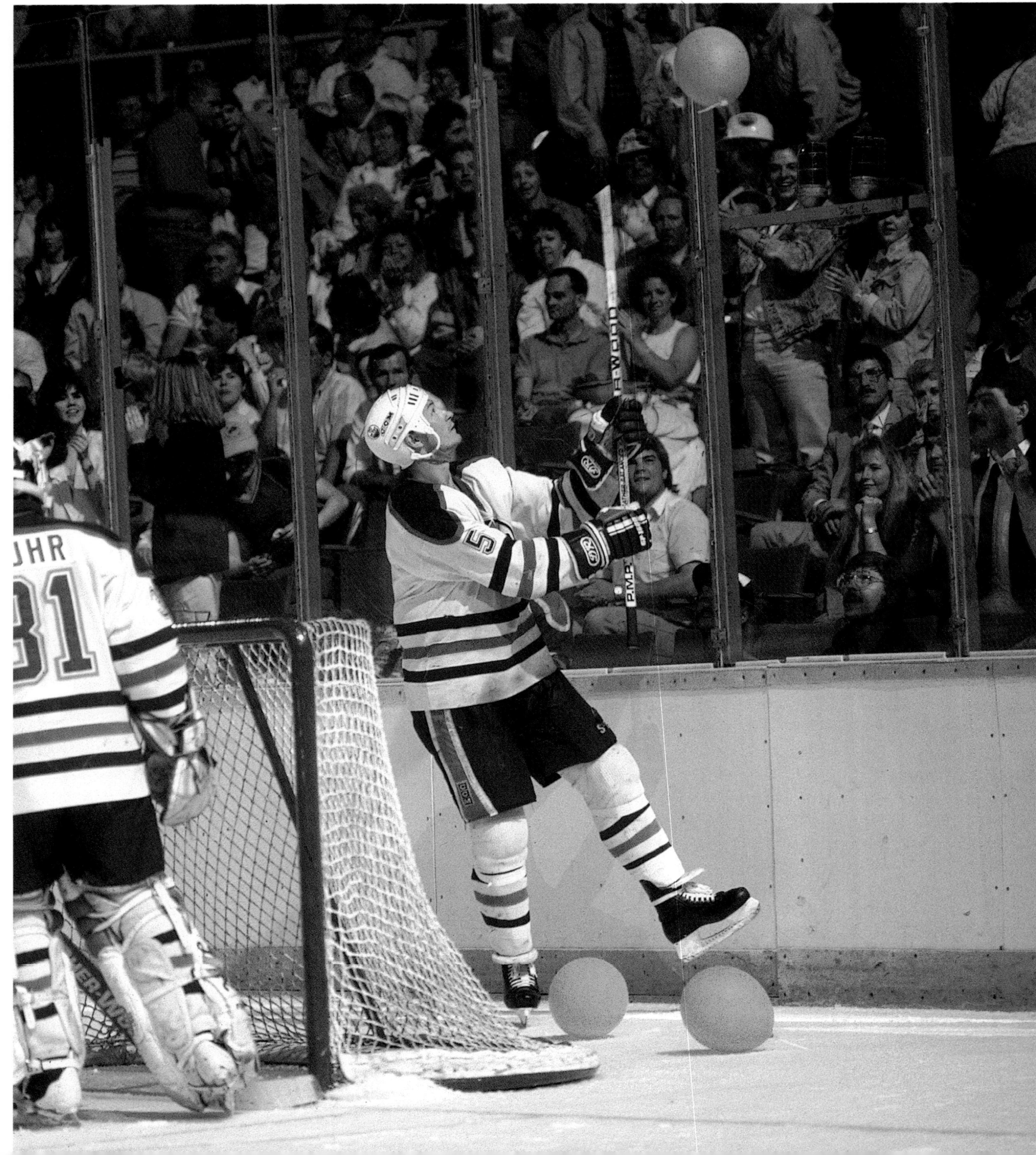
31
5
P.M.P.

The Bruins were little more than token opposition in 1988 as the Edmonton Oilers made it with four Cups in five years. This was the series in which Game Four in Boston was postponed after a 4,000-volt electrical switch blew out, plunging Boston Garden into darkness.

OVERLEAF: Calgary Flames goalie Mike Vernon drops to the ice to make a save versus Montreal in the '89 finals. Vernon's sixteen postseason wins tied him with Grant Fuhr for most wins by a goalie in a playoff year. Calgary became the first team to win the Cup on Montreal Forum ice.

Stanley Cup. Calgary beat the Montreal Canadiens four games to two and—more significantly and less likely—became the first visiting team ever to win the Cup in the Montreal Forum. MacInnis joined Serge Savard (1968), Bobby Orr (1970 and 1972) and Larry Robinson (1978) as the first defensemen to win the Conn Smythe Trophy. But it was Calgary right wing Lanny McDonald, he of the dragoon's mustache and hair so flaming red it looked like part of the team's logo, who seemed to personify his city's joy. After missing

Oiler defenseman Steve Smith could afford to play with balloons in the 1988 finals. Smith—the goat of the 1986 finals when his errant puck bounced into his own net, effectively eliminating Edmonton—would bounce back to be a mainstay in the Oilers '87, '88 and '90 Cup wins.

FLAMES
CCM
CANADIEN

entide
FLAMES
Cellulaire

18
NIKE

Oiler Craig Simpson gives Bruin legend Ray Bourque an unceremonious shove out of the Boston crease in 1988 just as Edmonton would shove the scrappy but outgunned Bs out of the playoffs 4–0.

Games Three, Four and Five, McDonald came back to score Calgary's second goal in a 4–2 Cup-clinching win. After a smiling McDonald had raised the Cup high over his head, a reporter asked him if it was heavy. "It's not heavy when you win it," said McDonald. "A guy could carry it all day."

But the Flames only carried the Cup for a year before the Oilers hauled it north on Highway 2 to Edmonton. Calgary never made it past the 1990 division semifinals, wherein they were eliminated in six games by Wayne Gretzky and the Kings. This set up Gretzky's return to Edmonton for a Kings-Oilers division final, in which the battered Kings—nine players were injured, including Gretzky who hurt his back after a Steve Smith hit in Game Three—were swept by a combined score of 24–10.

The Oilers went on to eliminate Chicago and once again meet Boston (winners over Hartford, Montreal and Washington) in the finals. The story line in Boston centered on whether or not Bruins captain Ray Bourque would continue the dubious distinction of being one of the best players never to have his name on the Cup. In Edmonton, the story line was whether or not the Oilers could win a Cup without Gretzky. Game One turned into the longest game in Stanley Cup finals history with the teams battling through 55:13 of overtime before seldom-used forward Petr Klima scored in what amounted to the sixth period, giving Edmonton a 3–2 win. The Oilers took three of the next four and won the Cup on Boston Garden ice with goalie Bill Ranford, who posted all of his team's sixteen playoff wins, getting the Conn Smythe Trophy.

This was the fifth Cup in seven years for the Oilers' Glenn Anderson, Grant Fuhr, Randy Gregg, Charlie Huddy, Jari Kurri, Kevin Lowe and Mark Messier. And though no one knew it, it would also be the end of the NHL's last true dynasty. Gretzky, watching the finals on television, said, "I would have liked it to be my team lifting the Cup. But those guys were my second choice."

In 1991, neither Gretzky's first or second choice played a part in the Cup finals. Instead, Mario Lemieux's Penguins skated to the fore. In French, Lemieux means "the best," and when Mario Lemieux was drafted first in 1984 by Pittsburgh, the NHL's worst team, he came into the league with more publicity than any rookie since Guy Lafleur. Then Minnesota North Stars GM Lou Nanne

Calgary's Doug Gilmour celebrates a Flames goal on Montreal goaltender Patrick Roy as Canadiens defenseman Chris Chelios does some tidy (if tardy) housecleaning in front of the Habs' cage in the 1989 finals, won by Calgary.

offered all twelve of his draft picks for Lemieux. No deal. But six years later it was Minnesota and Lemieux's resurgent Penguins competing in the Stanley Cup final.

Minnesota—sixteenth-place finisher in the regular season—pulled off one of the biggest first-round upsets in playoff history by dumping Chicago four games to two and continuing their surprising

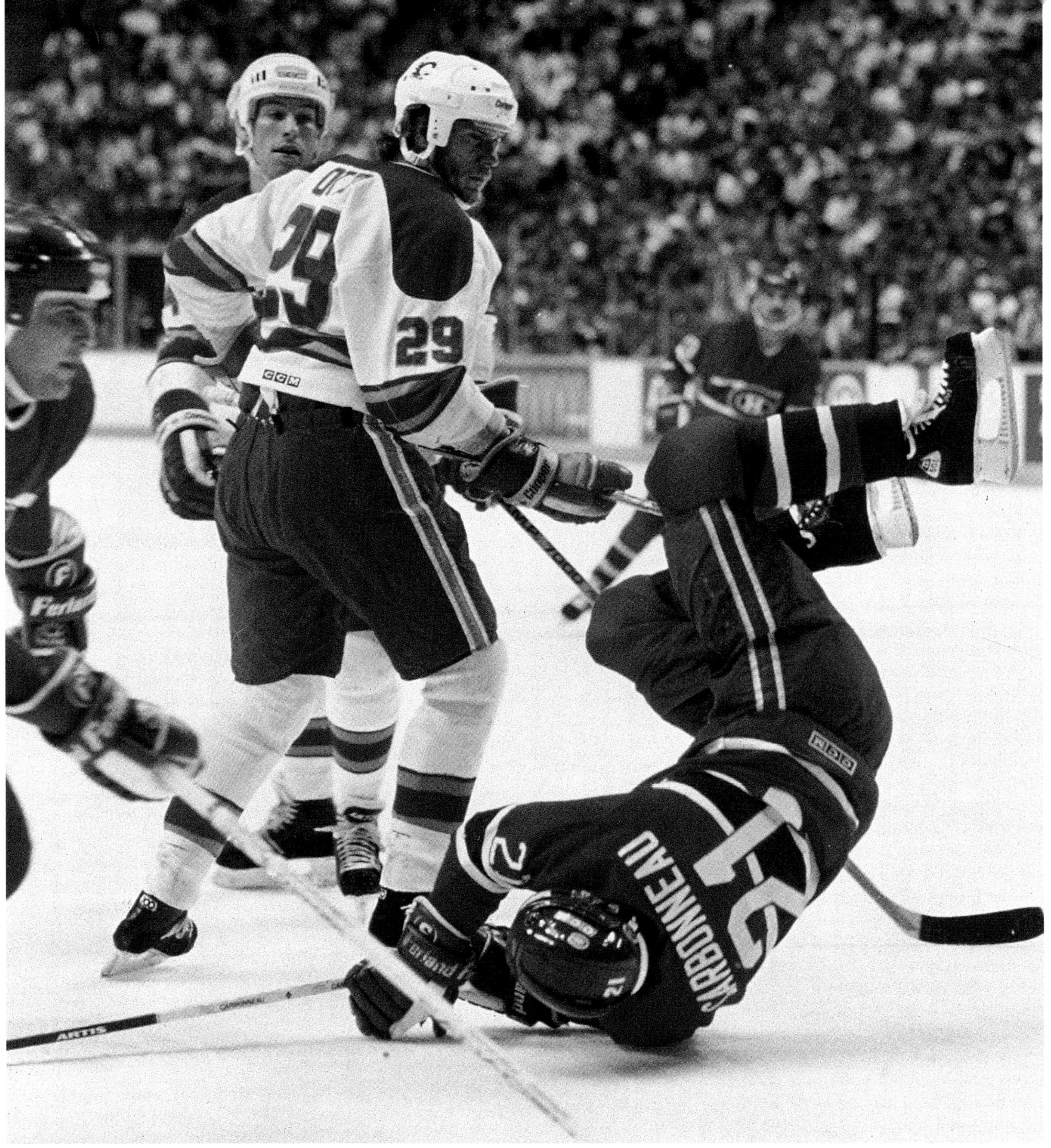

The Flames' Joel Otto dumps the Canadiens' veteran Guy Carbonneau in the 1989 finals wherein Calgary won the Cup and thus gained a measure of revenge over Montreal, who had beaten the Flames in the '86 finals.

Canadiens center Bobby Smith is slammed to the ice in the 1989 finals. Smith's three goals in the series led the Habs but there was no dousing the Flames en route to their first—and so far, only—Stanley Cup win.

march to the finals with wins over St. Louis and defending Cup champ Edmonton. Meanwhile Lemieux, a man who shrank from the spotlight while he burned out the goal light, led Pittsburgh past New Jersey, Washington and Boston. Behind the gritty goaltending of Tom Barrasso—who played the final two playoff rounds with an injured shoulder—the steady play of defenseman Larry Murphy (one goal, nine assists, ten points in the finals) and the scoring of Lemieux (five goals, seven assists, twelve points, despite missing one game with a bad back), the Pens won their first Stanley Cup and Lemieux took home the Conn Smythe Trophy.

Said the Pens' Phil Bourque after the win: "To see and feel the Cup, to pick it up, to hold it—that's the greatest feeling I've ever had." It was one he would have again though it would be tinged with sorrow.

While the Penguins savored their victory in the off-season, circumstances changed dramatically as the 1991–92 preseason

Goaltending immortal-in-embroyo Patrick Roy—he of the butterfly style and money game rep—rejoined the ranks of mere mortals in 1989 when his 2.58 GAA was respectable but not good enough to stop the Calgary Flames.

approached, especially for one of the team's most positive influences. "It's a great day for hockey," the relentlessly chipper Pittsburgh coach Bob Johnson said almost every day of his professional life. But it was far from a great day when, in September 1991, Johnson was diagnosed with brain cancer. He died a few weeks later. In a curious way, the upbeat Johnson seemed the perfect counterbalance to the somber and removed Lemieux, hockey's most unreachable star. But when Johnson's place was taken by the man who would become the NHL's greatest coach—the brilliant if inscrutable William Scotty Bowman—Lemieux and the

Edmonton captain Mark Messier moves in on ex-Oiler teammate Andy Moog in the 1990 finals versus the Bruins. This year the Oilers won their fifth Stanley Cup in seven years—their first since the 1988 trade of Wayne Gretzky to Los Angeles.

Bruins netminder Andy Moog topples into the Boston net in an effort to stop Mark Messier on a wraparound attempt in 1990. Edmonton's victory gave Messier and teammates Glenn Anderson, Grant Fuhr, Randy Gregg, Charlie Huddy, Jari Kurri and Kevin Lowe their fifth Cup ring as members of the Oilers.

MESSIER
11
11
CCM
SHER-WOOD

DIA
BRI
AFTER SHAVE • AFTER
Cooper
20
VAUGHN

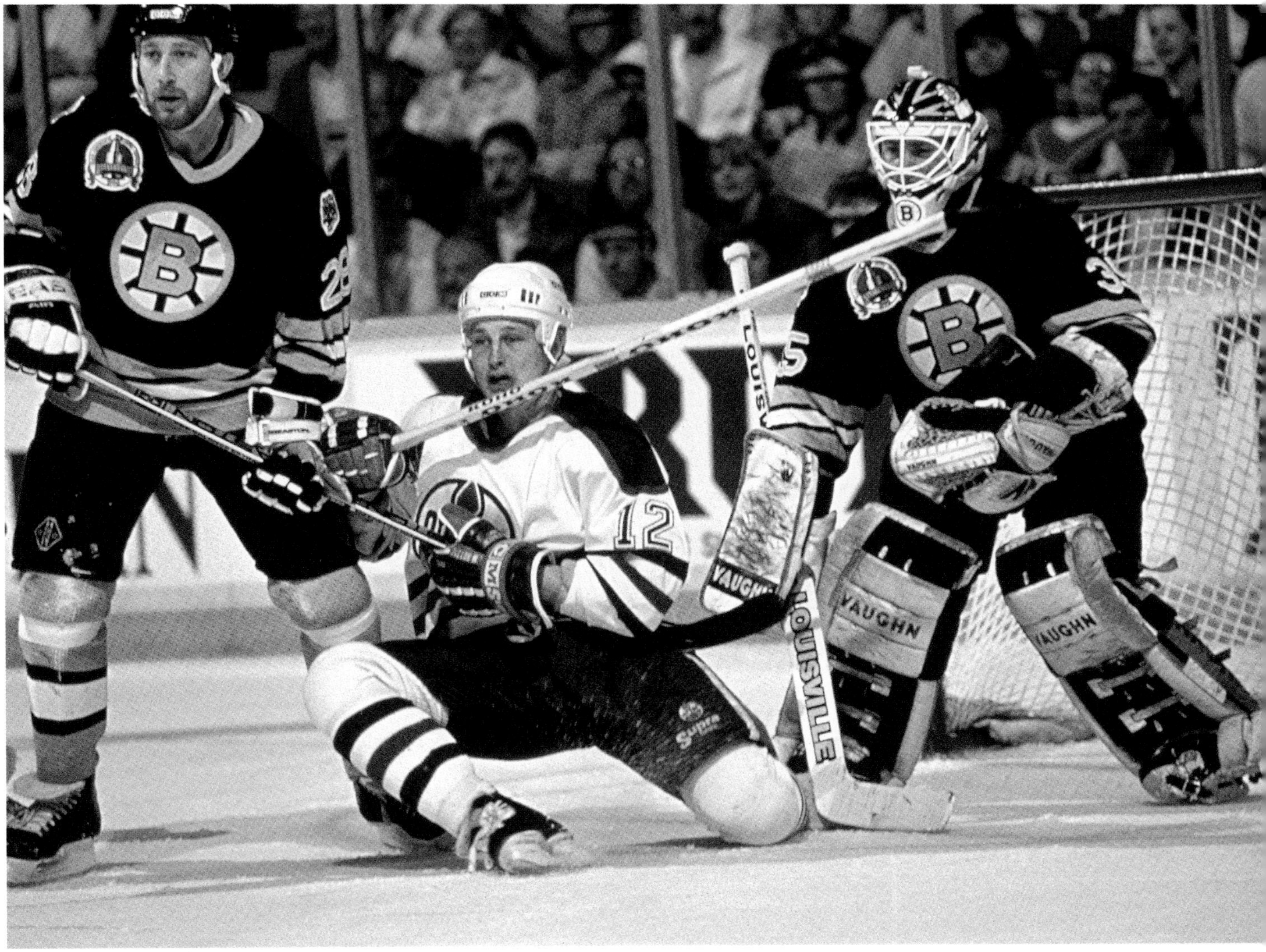

Bruins defenseman Garry Galley and goalie Andy Moog bracket falling Edmonton forward Adam Graves, but Graves and the Oilers would prove too much for the plucky Bs in 1990, the last year either team reached the finals.

Edmonton's Martin Gelinas is stopped by Boston goalie Andy Moog in the 1990 finals. Two years earlier, Moog left the Oilers in a dispute over salary and playing time and, following a year with Canada's national team, became the Bruins number one goalie.

Pittsburgh goalie Frank Pietrangelo, subbing for injured starter Tom Barrasso, stops a Minnesota shot in the 1991 finals, won in six games by the Penguins for the first of their two consecutive Stanley Cups.

Penguin teenager Jaromir Jagr—who would later emerge from the shadow of teammate Mario Lemieux to claim a superstardom of his own—here hustles back on defense in the 1991 finals in which he was goalless but had five assists.

OVERLEAF: Pittsburgh's Jaromir Jagr is stopped during the '91 finals by North Stars goalie Jon Casey as defenseman Jim Johnson moves in with assistance. Helping the North Stars reach the finals was the monster upset of defending champ Edmonton in the Conference finals.

Gulf
CHRISTIAN
30
CCM
CHRISTIAN

CCM
JAGR
68
JOHNSON
8
VICTOR

Jaromir Jagr wades into a trio of North Stars in Game Three of the 1991 finals. Jagr finished his first playoffs with a respectable three goals and ten assists, for thirteen points. But he would explode with twenty-six points (eleven goals) in the next year's postseason play.

Pittsburgh's Ron Francis slices between Chicago goaltender Eddie Belfour and the backchecking Michel Goulet (16) in the 1992 finals. The Penguins swept the Blackhawks, who were making their first appearance in the finals since 1973.

Pens simply kept rolling into another Cup final versus Chicago, a team coached by Bowman's foremost and self-admitted admirer, Mike Keenan. The student would have one more lesson to learn.

The Blackhawks entered the finals having established a new NHL record for consecutive playoff wins with eleven. The Pens came in playing a slightly more defensive style under Bowman than they had under Johnson and with Lemieux nursing a broken hand as a result of Ranger Adam Graves' slash in a first-round game. Graves got a four-game suspension for the hit; Lemieux missed six playoff games with the injury. In Game One, the Hawks blew a 4–1 lead as Pittsburgh's Jaromir Jagr scored a spectacular tying goal, stickhandling around two defenders and beating Ed Belfour with a backhander. There were only thirteen seconds left when Lemieux scored the game winner and the broom was out of the closet. Pittsburgh closed it out 3–1, 1–0 and 6–5, and dedicated the team's second Stanley Cup to Johnson who, said Lemieux, "taught us how to win."

Lemieux again—despite missing those six games—won the Conn Smythe Trophy to join ex-Flyer goalie Bernie Parent (1974–75) as only the second player in NHL history to win back-to-back playoff MVP awards. In fifteen games Lemieux scored five game-winning goals.

The 1990s produced the NHL's second golden age of goaltenders. By 1993, a generation's worth of better coaching, equipment and conditioning was producing a corps of elite netminders such as Patrick Roy, Mike Richter, Grant Fuhr, Dominik Hasek, Felix Potvin, Eddie Belfour and Curtis Joseph—a group to rival the late-1950s and early-1960s first golden age of goalies dominated by Terry Sawchuk, Jacques Plante, Glenn Hall, Johnny Bower and Gump Worsley. Save percentages improved from .870 in 1987 to better than .900 by 1993. Small wonder that games got tighter. Indeed, of eighty-five games played in the 1993 playoffs, a record twenty-eight went into overtime, shattering the previous records of sixteen set in 1982 and 1991. "It used to be that a few teams had a great goalie," said TV analyst and ex-NHL goalie John Davidson, "now there are few who don't."

But the star that burned brightest in the 1993 playoffs was Montreal's Roy. After losing a first-round overtime game 3–2 to

In 1992 Pittsburgh captain Mario Lemieux, shown above launching a backhand pass, joined ex-Philadelphia goalie Bernie Parent as only the second player in NHL history to win back-to-back playoff MVP awards.

HASEK
31

Goalie Dominik Hasek was little more than a spare for Chicago in the 1992 playoffs, where he was 0–2 with a modest 3.04 GAA and .886 save percentage. Few knew that the acrobatic Hasek would go on to become one of the great goalies of all time.

Gulf
WE KNOW
ROENICK
27
CCM

Pittsburgh goalie Tom Barrasso catches a Chicago shot in the 1992 finals. Barrasso was in net for all of the Penguins postseason wins, picking up a record of 16–5 with a 2.82 GAA and .907 save percentage.

Quebec, Roy reeled off an astonishing seven overtime victories—two versus Quebec, three in a row as Montreal swept Buffalo and two in a row versus the Islanders—as Montreal fought its way to the finals where they faced Wayne Gretzky's Los Angeles Kings (winners over Calgary, Vancouver and Toronto) in a series matching the game's greatest scorer against its then greatest goalie. Gretzky won the first round when he figured in every L.A. goal (scoring one, assisting on three) in a 4–1 opening-game win at Montreal. But then Roy and the Habs took over, winning three consecutive overtime games before clinching the franchise's twenty-fourth Cup with a 4–1 win in Montreal. It would be the last Stanley Cup they would win in the Forum.

Roy's 16–4 record, 2.14 goals against average and record ten overtime wins won him his second Conn Smythe Trophy and—until Hasek's back-to-back Hart Trophies in 1997 and 1998—established him as the best in a glittering group of golden goalies.

While Lemieux carved his signature across the 1990s and Gretzky continued putting up video arcade numbers in L.A., it was the engaging and belligerent New York Ranger captain Mark Messier who would emerge in 1994 as the greatest on-ice leader since Bobby Clarke. Messier took his bellicose act to Broadway in 1991—the result of an Edmonton–New York trade—and in just three seasons jammed some steel up the spines of the

The L.A. Kings' Wayne Gretzky raises his arms in celebration of Luc Robitaille's goal on Montreal's Patrick Roy in the 1993 finals. But the final celebration went to Club de Hockey Canadien as they eliminated the Kings in five games.

heretofore wimpy Rangers. Following New York wins over the Islanders and Capitals, the Rangers trailed New Jersey three games to two in the conference finals when Messier provided one of the defining moments in his career and in playoff history. In a gesture reminiscent of Broadway Joe Namath's "guarantee" of a Jets victory in the NFL's Super Bowl III, Messier told the media, "I know we're going to go in [to New Jersey] and win Game Six and bring it back here for Game Seven. When Messier produced a hat trick to power the Rangers to a 4–2 Game Six win and after the Rangers clinched the series 2–1 in overtime in Game Seven, Broadway Mark had joined Broadway Joe as an icon of the brash New York sports culture. "I had to do something to instill the old confidence ... I didn't care about the consequences," said Messier.

The most obvious consequence was that the Rangers met the Vancouver Canucks, winners over Calgary, Dallas and Toronto, in a Cup final that went seven games before the Rangers won it 3–2 in Madison Square Garden, ending the team's fifty-four-year Stanley Cup drought and silencing derisive fan chants of "1940, 1940," that being the last year the Rangers had won the Cup. New York defenseman Brian Leetch—who led all playoff scorers with eleven goals and twenty-three assists for thirty-four points in twenty-three games—became the first U.S.-born player to win the Conn Smythe Trophy while New York coach Mike Keenan won his first Cup in four trips to the finals. As the Rangers paraded around Madison Square Garden a fan held up a sign that read: "Now I can die happy."

New York's happiness came to an end the next season, as the once new age of swirling high-speed hockey begun by the Edmonton Oilers in 1984 came to an end in 1995 when stifling neutral zone defenses threw a tactical blanket over wide-open offenses. Speed may kill, but not if it can't get through center ice.

The best of the trap lines was strung out by New Jersey's Devils, coached by ex-Montreal great Jacques Lemaire, whose main philosophy was: the first step to winning a game is making sure you don't lose it. The Devils lost only four games in the first three rounds as they suffocated the Bruins, Penguins and Flyers. What the trap didn't stop, Devils goalie Martin Brodeur did. Meanwhile, the Red Wings put on an even stronger showing, losing only twice in series victories over the Stars, Sharks and Blackhawks. But when

Cooper
CCM
SHER-WOOD
KOHO

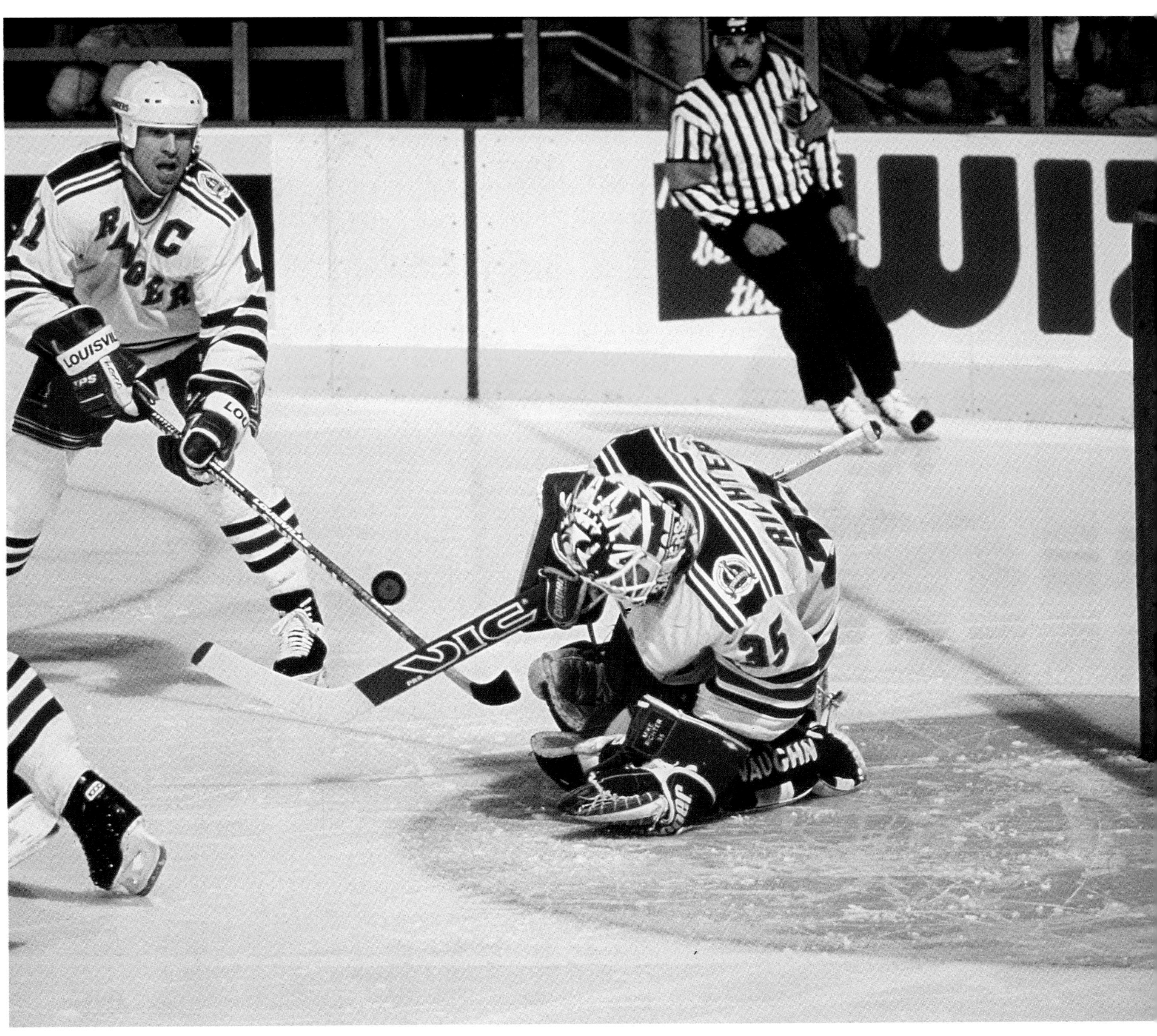

Montreal goalie Patrick Roy played like the "St. Patrick" of the eighties versus the Kings in the 1993 finals. Roy won the Conn Smythe Trophy and his 16–4 final record included an astonishing ten overtime victories.

New York Ranger goalie Mike Richter makes a save and captain Mark Messier—the 1994 Conn Smythe Trophy winner—moves to clear the rebound as the Rangers ended their fifty-four-year Cup drought, beating Vancouver in seven games.

New York's Mark Messier celebrates the Cup-clinching goal over the Canucks in 1994. Earlier, Messier became part of playoff lore when he "guaranteed" a Ranger win and backed it up with a hat trick as New York faced possible semifinal elimination by New Jersey.

Pavel Bure, Vancouver's "Russian Rocket," fizzled on this scoring attempt against the Rangers' Mike Richter in 1994. Bure led the Canucks in final-round scoring with three goals and eight points, but it wasn't enough to stop New York.

Life
Sea
35
Cooper
VIC

Goalie Mike Richter and teammate Steve Larmer defend the Rangers net versus Vancouver in the 1994 finals. Richter played in all seven final-round games, posting a solid 2.60 GAA and coming up with the big save when his team needed it.

New Jersey met Detroit, it wasn't even close. The Devils gave up only seven goals in a coldly efficient four-game sweep for the franchise's first Stanley Cup. "We gave the Red Wings and those other teams nothing," said New Jersey defenseman Scott Stevens. No one argued.

Devils forward Claude Lemieux, who scored only six goals in the regular season, exploded for thirteen in the playoffs and was awarded the Conn Smythe Trophy, adding to his reputation as one of the NHL's best "money" players.

In 1996, a team was reborn in the winter of its seventeenth year. It was bitter irony for the hockey fans of Quebec City when this team—who for sixteen Cup-less seasons operated as the Quebec Nordiques—relocated to Denver for the 1995–96 season as the Colorado Avalanche and immediately won the Stanley Cup.

The Avalanche rode the best one-two center combination in the world—Joe Sakic and Peter Forsberg—the goaltending of Patrick Roy, acquired in a trade from Montreal, and the get-under-their-skin style of ex–New Jersey playoff hero Claude Lemieux to take consecutive 4–2 series wins over Vancouver, Chicago and Detroit, before sweeping the surprising Florida Panthers in four straight. Florida reached the finals largely on the brilliant goaltending of John "Beezer" Vanbiesbrouck. The Beezer backstopped the third-year Panthers to eliminations of Boston, Philadelphia and Pittsburgh.

The fourth and last game of the final series was literally one for the record books as defenseman Uwe Krupp scored at 4:31 of the third overtime period on the 119th shot of the game in the longest 1–0 overtime playoff game since 1936, when Detroit shut out the Montreal Maroons in six overtimes. Sakic (eighteen goals, thirty-four

The New Jersey net and goaltender Martin Brodeur were well defended in 1995 as the Devils—following twenty-one years and two franchise relocations—won their first Stanley Cup in a shocking sweep of the favored Detroit Red Wings.

points) took home the Conn Smythe Trophy, Roy took another step in establishing himself as one of the greatest goalies in NHL history and Colorado's new fans went on a Rocky Mountain high. Fans in Quebec were on something less than that.

In 1997, the Red Wings hadn't won a Cup since 1955 and the days of Gordie Howe. Worse—or so it must have seemed to a generation of Motown hockey fans—Detroit had an eight-game home losing streak in Stanley Cup finals. But all was forgotten and forgiven on June 7, when coach Scotty Bowman won his seventh Stanley Cup with his third team. Bowman's Wings earned their trip to the finals with walk-in-the-park ease, eliminating St. Louis four games to two, sweeping Anaheim and dumping defending champion Colorado four games to two. Yet the hot Wings were heavy underdogs as they went up against the supposedly bigger, tougher

Flyers (winners over the Penguins, Sabres and Rangers) in the finals. But here, Detroit—paced by Nicklas Lidstrom's defense and Mike Vernon's goaltending (Vernon allowed two goals or fewer in seventeen of his twenty playoff appearances)—opened with a pair of 4–2 wins in Philly before hammering the Flyers 6–1 in Motown. The one-sidedness of that loss provoked Flyer coach Terry Murray to say his team was in a "choking situation." That the comment annoyed Murray's players and angered Philly management doesn't mean it wasn't true. Goals by Lidstrom and Darren McCarty gave the Wings a 2–1 Cup-clinching win and put Philly in a golfing situation. Vernon's 1.76 playoff goals against average was enough to earn him the Conn Smythe Trophy. Steve Yzerman raised the Cup in Joe Louis Arena, and the octopus-tossing citizens of Hockey Town were in ecstasy.

Detroit's Sergei Fedorov can't leap through a trio of Devils that includes defensemen Scott Stevens (4) and Scott Niedermayer (27) in the '95 finals. Stevens was then in the process of solidifying his reputation as one of the best hitters in NHL history.

Detroit defenseman Nicklas Lidstrom keeps New Jersey's Neal Broten from moving in on the Devils' goal in Game One of the '95 finals. Detroit would need more defense than this as New Jersey outscored them 16–7 for the series, en route to hoisting the Cup.

The veteran-laden Stanley Cup champion Red Wings, third-place finishers overall in 1997–98, looked at times like the over-the-hill gang as they lurched to the Stanley Cup finals in consecutive and closely contested six-game series wins over Phoenix, St. Louis and Colorado. In the East, the surprising Washington Capitals rode the goaltending of Olaf Kolzig—a.k.a. "Ollie the Goalie"—to their first Cup final via wins over Boston, Ottawa and Buffalo (in which

Devils goalie Martin Brodeur strengthened his case as one of the great goalies of his era in the 1995 playoffs. Brodeur racked up a 1.67 GAA for the playoffs (1.75 in the finals) playing brilliantly and benefiting from the Devils' suffocating neutral zone defense.

Kolzig outdueled Dominik Hasek) to carry a 1.69 goals against average into the last round.

But in the Wings' four-game sweep of the Caps, it was the heretofore oft-maligned Detroit goalie Chris Osgood who played like the Wizard of Oz, backstopping the Wings to nail-biter wins of 2–1, 5–4 (in overtime) and 2–1 before the almost anticlimactic 4–1 Detroit clincher in Washington.

OVERLEAF: In the 1996 finals the Colorado Avalanche pushed aside the upstart Florida Panthers in four straight. Adam Deadmarsh (52) had seventeen points (five goals) in twenty-two playoff games. His four assists against Florida ranked him third behind superstars Joe Sakic and Peter Forsberg in finals scoring.

Cooper
EASTON
52

CCM
52

That victory marked the eighth Cup win for Detroit coach Scotty Bowman, tying him with Montreal legend Toe Blake as coaches with the most Stanley Cup rings. Red Wings captain Steve Yzerman was Motown's Stevie Wonder as his twenty-four points in twenty-two games earned him the Conn Smythe Trophy. However, Yzerman will be better remembered for one of the most gracefully transcendent gestures seen at an on-ice Cup celebration. Ex-Detroit defenseman Vladimir Konstantinov—almost fatally injured in the crash of a limousine a year earlier and at this point still in a wheelchair—was wheeled onto the ice after the Detroit win. Upon seeing Konstantinov, Yzerman—who would later say he'd intended to pass the Cup first to Osgood—impulsively passed it to the smiling man in the chair. "Not too often does a moment in hockey transcend sports," said Detroit forward Brendan Shanahan. Yzerman's act, so gracefully compassionate, will be remembered for as long as the Stanley Cup exists.

Death casts a long shadow and most of the 1999 playoffs were played in the dark aftermath of Carolina Hurricane defenseman Steve Chaisson's fatal accident. Chaisson was killed when his truck overturned as he was driving home from a team party following Boston's first-round upset of the Hurricanes.

Boston would go on to lose a second-round series to Buffalo, which played its way into the finals with a first-round sweep of Ottawa and a conference final win over Toronto. The best in the West—and the best team during the regular season—was Dallas, which reached the finals via wins over Edmonton, St. Louis and Colorado. The Stars were led by forwards Mike Modano and Joe Nieuwendyk, and goaltender Eddie "the Eagle" Belfour who outperformed Patrick Roy in the conference finals and then Dominik Hasek in the finals, as the aptly named Stars became the first team in five years to win both the Presidents' Trophy and the Stanley Cup. But the series ended on what Buffalo coach Lindy Ruff called "a worst nightmare scenario." With the Stars up three games to two and Game Six tied 1–1 deep in the third overtime at Buffalo, Dallas forward Brett Hull jammed a puck past Hasek and the Stars players poured onto the ice to celebrate the apparent Cup winner. However, TV replays showed Hull's skate was clearly in the crease, but the goal—while shown repeatedly to the television

Colorado's Joe Sakic scores on Florida's John Vanbiesbrouck in Game Three of the '96 finals. Sakic's thirty-four points (eighteen goals) led all playoff scorers and earned him the Conn Smythe Trophy.

audience—was not reviewed by officials. NHL director of officiating Bryan Lewis later said that there was not a crease violation because "Hull had possession of the puck when his left foot entered the crease." The replay seemed to show otherwise, but the controversial goal stood.

Said Hull after the game: "The world was lifted off my back with that goal, [now] I don't have to take any more crap about not being able to win the big game."

Modano had a monster playoff, leading the postseason with eighteen assists. Nieuwendyk—whose eleven postseason goals led the league—won the Conn Smythe Trophy. The Conn Smythe Trophy winner wasn't a great goal scorer, but he definitely was an impact player.

It's rare that a bodycheck becomes the defining moment in postseason play, but New Jersey defenseman and captain Scott

Colorado goaltender Patrick Roy and captain Joe Sakic fend off Florida's Rob Niedermayer in 1996 as the Avalanche became Stanley Cup champions in their first season in Denver since relocating from Quebec City.

Patrick Roy takes a headfirst dive in front of Colorado teammates Joe Sakic (19) and Sandis Ozolinsh (8) in 1996. Nominally a defenseman, Ozolinsh's five goals and 19 points contributed mightily to the Colorado offense.

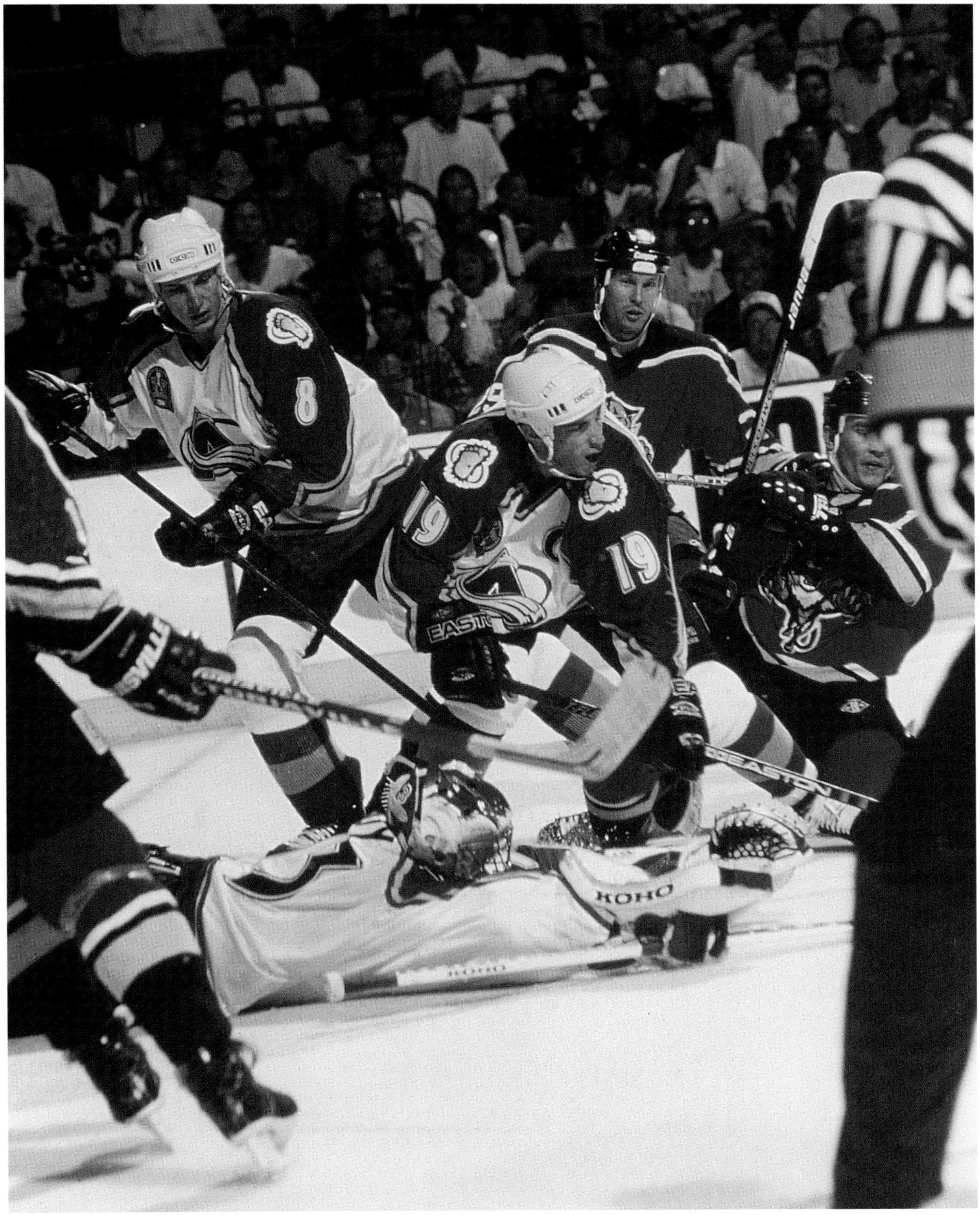

OVERLEAF: RATS!...Hundreds of toy rats litter the ice around Colorado goalie Patrick Roy in the '96 finals. After a rat (a real one) was spotted in the Florida dressing room—and quickly dispatched with a hockey stick—the little rodents became a sort of unofficial mascot for the Panthers and their rollicking fans.

Detroit's Darren McCarty (25) jostles aside Philadelphia's Dainius Zubrus in the '97 finals in which the Red Wings won their first Cup since 1955 and the Gordie Howe glory years. Detroit won in a sweep.

Speedy Detroit center Sergei Fedorov leaves a trail of bodies in his wake as he sprints to the puck in the 1997 finals. Fedorov scored twice in a 6–1 Wings win in Game Three at Joe Louis Arena. That victory snapped Detroit's eight-game, thirty-three-year home-ice losing streak in the Stanley Cup finals.

Flyer defenseman Eric Desjardins has his route to the Red Wings' net cut off by Detroit's backchecking Brendan Shanahan in 1997. Shanahan would finish the final series with three goals and four points to tie Steve Yzerman for second in team scoring, two points behind Detroit leader Sergei Fedorov.

DESJARDINS
37
Little Caesars
HOME OF PIZZA!PIZZA!
BAUER

Washington center Joe Juneau lays the lumber across the shoulders of Detroit captain Steve Yzerman in the '98 finals. The Wings swept the Caps and Yzerman's twenty-four points (six goals) and two-way play won him the Conn Smythe Trophy.

Detroit goalie Mike Vernon searches for the puck over the sprawled body of teammate Doug Brown and kneeling Philly veteran Rod Brind'Amour in 1997. Vernon would go on to win the Conn Smythe Trophy, finishing the playoffs with a 16–4 record and allowing fewer than two goals in seventeen of those twenty starts.

Stevens' open-ice, lights-out smackdown of Philadelphia center Eric Lindros in the Devils' 2–1 win in Game Seven of the Eastern Conference finals may well have been the play that put the Devils (earlier winners over Toronto and Florida) into the finals against defending champion Dallas. That check at the Devils blue line gave Lindros a concussion that put him out of that game, the playoffs and all of the next season. "I hated it," Stevens said of the publicity given the hit. "But it's playoff time and playoff time is war."

Defending Cup champion Dallas came into Stevens' "war" via wins over Edmonton, San Jose and Colorado. But Dallas would never score more than three goals in a game against New Jersey as Devils coach Larry Robinson—who replaced the fired Robbie Ftorek with eight games left in the regular season—stressed "responsible" team defense and resorted to the trap when the Devils held the lead. A defense anchored by Stevens, defensive partner Brian Rafalski and goalie Martin Brodeur (1.61 goals against average), and an attack paced by a youthful (average age twenty-four) first line of center Jason Arnott between Czech-born wingers Petr Sykora and Patrik Elias, snuffed out the Stars in six games. Arnott scored the Cup winner at 28:20 of overtime. Minutes after that goal, Stevens—who would be voted the Conn Smythe Trophy winner—took the silver bowl of the Stanley Cup in his right hand, the metal base in his left hand, raised the trophy high over his head, then lowered it to his mouth … and kissed it. It was a gesture born more of love than of war.

OVERLEAF: Detroit's Tomas Holmstrom scores despite being surrounded by Caps in the 1998 finals. Detroit's win in this series gave Wings' coach Scotty Bowman his eighth Stanley Cup as an NHL head coach, tying him with Montreal coaching legend Toe Blake.

Detroit center Sergei Fedorov races past Washington's frantically pokechecking Andrei Nikolishin as the Caps' Peter Bondra looks on. Fedorov had a goal and two assists in the Red Wings' sweep.

Pesky Washington Capitals forward Esa Tikkanen slices between Detroit's Kirk Maltby (left) and Jamie Macoun only to be stopped by the outstretched arm and stick of Red Wings goaltender Chris Osgood in the 1998 finals.

Buffalo's Joe Juneau tries his hand at goaltending as goalie Dominik Hasek is pinned to the ice and teammate Erik Rasmussen is blocked from the crease in the '99 finals. Dallas won the series in six games, making it the first time since 1994 that the finals did not end in a sweep.

The Dallas Stars' Pat Verbeek is sandwiched between Sabres goalie Dominik Hasek and Richard Smehlik in the 1999 finals. Verbeek finished the playoffs with seven points (three goals) including a goal in the Buffalo series during his team's victorious run to the Cup.

SMEHLIK
42
16
BAUER

Buffalo's Geoff Sanderson stickhandles around Dallas goalie Eddie Belfour in the '99 finals. The Stars won the series with Belfour outplaying his more celebrated goaltending rival Dominik Hasek. Belfour recorded a remarkable 1.26 GAA in the finals to Hasek's good (but not quite good enough) 1.68.

Sabres netminder Dominik "the Dominator" Hasek stacks the pads to stop this Dallas drive in the 1999 finals. But not even the acrobatic work of two-time league MVP (1997 and 1998) Hasek could stop the Stars.

HASEK
39
39
BAUER
BAUER

The Stars' Brett Hull—a.k.a. the "Golden Jet"—moves in on Dominik Hasek in '99. Hull scored three goals in the finals, including the series winner. Said Hull after his Cup-clinching goal in triple overtime, "The world was lifted off my back with that goal."

VAUGHN

The Stars' Pat Verbeek pops a backhander past Buffalo goalie Dominik Hasek as down-and-out-of-the-play Sabres defenseman Rhett Warrener looks on helplessly in the '99 finals.

Eddie the "Eagle" Belfour—here pouncing on a loose puck—was flying high in the 1999 playoffs as he had in the regular season. Belfour's season-long steady play was a big reason the Stars became the first team in five years to win both the President's Trophy as the best team in the regular season plus the Stanley Cup.

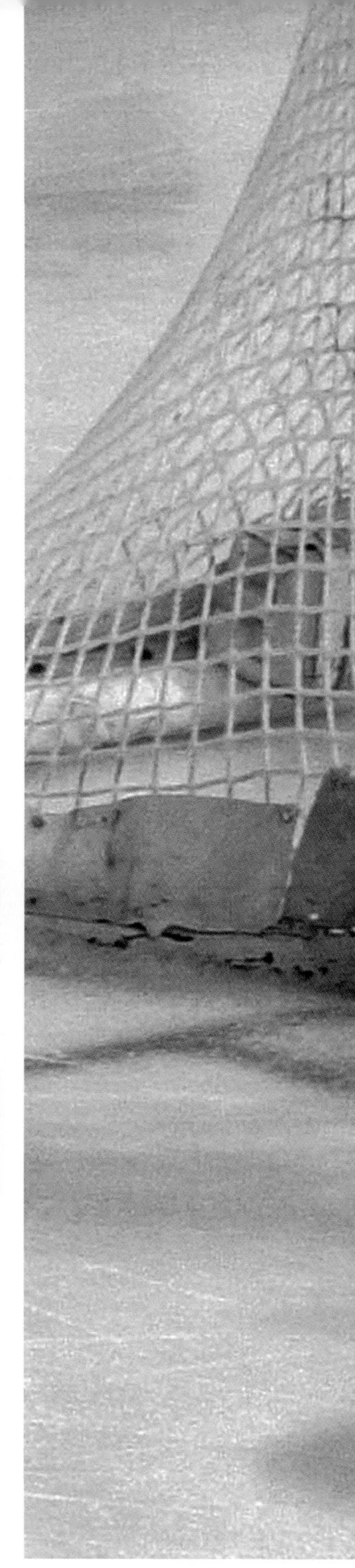

The Eagle has crash landed—Eddie Belfour can only watch helplessly as this New Jersey shot sails into the Dallas net in the 2000 finals. This goal notwithstanding, Belfour had a strong playoff with fourteen wins, four shutouts and a 1.87 GAA. But it wasn't enough to stop New Jersey.

New Jersey goaltender Martin Brodeur drops to the ice to stop this shot by Dallas Stars center Kirk Muller in the 2000 finals. Brodeur—with his 1.61 playoff GAA—was a big factor in the Devils lugging the Cup back to New Jersey Turnpike Exit 16W.

LEGACY

Martin Brodeur stays on his feet to deny an onrushing Brett Hull (16) who is pressured from behind by Devils captain and soon-to-be playoff MVP Scott Stevens. The defining moment of the 2000 playoffs may have been Stevens's lights-out bodycheck of Philadelphia captain Eric Lindros in the Eastern Conference finals.

Dallas star Mike Modano looks more like "Air" Modano as he goes hurtling over Devils goalie Martin Brodeur in the 2000 finals. Modano's twenty-three points (ten goals) was second to teammate Brett Hull's twenty-four (eleven goals) among all playoff scorers. But that wasn't enough to keep the Devils from wresting the Cup from the defending champs.

DALLAS
STARS

New Jersey left wing John Madden scores against the Stars' Eddie Belfour in the 2000 finals. Madden, who had just turned twenty-five, was one of a group of young players—including more heralded teammates Petr Sykora and Patrik Elias—whose play was a big factor in the Devils winning the Cup.

2000-2001 Stanley Cup Final

Joe Sakic (right) celebrates as he scores on the Devils' Martin Brodeur during the second period of game one. Crashing into Brodeur is teammate Petr Sykora. The Avs buried the Devils 5-0 in the opening game.

No one in 109 years had phrased a player's quest for the Cup better than Bill Torrey did after Game Five of the 2001 finals. "Unfortunately, no player is owed a Cup," said the Florida GM and former architect of the New York Islanders 1980-83 dynasty, "But several players deserve one and Ray Bourque is one of those players."

Torrey said that with the defending champion New Jersey Devils up three games to two on the Colorado Avalanche and 40-year old defenseman and five-time Norris Trophy winner Bourque rumored to be in his final season and seemingly likely to wear forever the label of best player never to win a Cup.

For one of the few times in playoff history the main story line of the finals focused as much on a player as on a team.

But in Game Six in New Jersey, Avalanche goaltender Patrick Roy, whose mishandling of the puck in Game Four arguably cost his team a win and a 3-1 series lead, shutout the Devils 4-0 in New Jersey to force what was only the fourth Game Seven final in the post-expansion era.

Two goals by Colorado's Alex Tanguay, a power play goal by Colorado captain Joe Sakic, and the almost seamless goaltending of Conn Smythe Trophy winner Roy (forty-nine saves on fifty shots in Game Six and Seven) brought Colorado—and Bourque—the coveted thirty-two-pound chalice.

Sakic, taking the trophy from NHL Commissioner Gary Bettman, passed up the captain's traditional skate around the arena and instead handed the Cup immediately to Bourque. Smiling and crying at the same time, Bourque lifted the trophy over his head as shouts of "Ray...Ray...Ray..." came down from the stands. "It's just such a weird feeling after all this time," said Bourque. "You don't know how you're going to feel when it finally happens, then all of a sudden there were all these different feelings of joy...I was just floating. Finally, it happened."

"A name was missing from that thing," said Roy of the Cup and of his teammate. "And today it is back to normal."

But the final word on the Cup belonged to Bourque who, following the Avalanche's victory parade through the streets of Denver, may have been speaking for all Cup winners of the last 109 years when he said: "Knowing that I'll have this feeling for a long, long time—that's the best part of all."

New Jersey's Turner Stevenson (right) battles for the puck with Colorado's Martin Skoula during the third period of game two. The Devils avenged their game one thrashing by beating the Avalanche 2-1.

Devils' goaltender Martin Brodeur (right) is sent flying by a hit from the Avalanche's Dan Hinote during the first period of game two.

New Jersey's Alexander Moligny crashes into Colorado's goaltender Patrick Roy as the Martin Skoula tries to haul him down during the second period of game two in Denver.

Martin Brodeur makes a nifty save on Colorado's Adam Foote during second period action in game three of the finals. The Avs won the game 3-1 to take a 2-1 lead in the series.

The Avs Chris Drury scores the team's second goal on the Devils' Martin Brodeur during the second period of game four in New Jersey. The Devils' 3-2 come-from-behind win evened the best-of-seven finals at two games a piece.

Colin White and Petr Sykora sandwich Colorado's Eric Messier during third period action in game four of the playoffs.

Martin Brodeur dives to make the save on Colorado's Dave Reid during the first period of game five. New Jersey won a convincing 4-1 game over the Avalanche to take a 3-2 lead in the series.

OVERLEAF: Patrick Roy is a little too late on a shot by Patrick Elias during the first period of game five.

KOHO
KOHO

Patrick Roy juggles the puck and makes the save during the first period of game five in Denver.

New Jersey's Bobby Holik knocks Patrick Roy into the net during the spirited first period of game six. Colorado tied the series 3-3 after a decisive 4-0 trouncing of the Devils in New Jersey.

Alex Tanguay moves around the net and scores his first of two goals during game seven of the finals.

The Avalanche's Alex Tanguay scores his second goal of the night against Martin Brodeur during the second period of game seven in Denver. Winning 3-1, the Avs brought home the Cup for the second time in five years.

Joe Sakic is knocked into Martin Brodeur by Ken Daneyko during the first period of game seven.

Ray Bourque gets a congratulatory kiss from teammate Dave Reid after beating the Devils and winning the Stanley Cup. Bourque's dream of hoisting the Cup before his retirement finally came true with the Avs 3-1 win over the Devils.

Celebration

NHL President Frank Calder has just presented the 1933 Stanley Cup to the New York Rangers, it was New York's second Cup in seven years.

Jubilant New York Rangers players and officials gather round the 1940 Cup, the last the Rangers would win for a frustrating 54 years, with "Nineteen Forty...Nineteen Forty" becoming a chant of derision until New York won the Cup again in 1994.

Toronto's Nick Metz, Wally Stankowski and Don Metz admire the 1942 Cup the Leafs had just won from Detroit.

The Detroit Red Wings surround the now re-designed Stanley Cup. Many of the older "collars" listing player names were removed and taken into safekeeping so that the trophy would remain of manageable size. No. 9 at right is Detroit superstar Gordie Howe.

Detroit goalie Terry Sawchuck (left) and captain Sid Abel pucker up with the 1952 Stanley Cup.

Canadiens coach Toe Blake, hanging on the shoulders of Butch Bouchard, prepares to drink from the 1956 Cup. Blake and Montreal would slake their thirst for championships a league record five consecutive times, from 1956 to 1960.

Montreal goalie Jacques Plante and captain Maurice "the Rocket" Richard grasp the 1960 Cup, the last the two Hall of Famers would win together. Richard retired the next season and Plante was traded to New York before the Habs won their next Cup in 1968.

Chicago's Golden Jet, Bobby Hull (left), and jut-jawed teammate Jack Evans with the 1961 Stanley Cup, the first the Black Hawks had won since 1938 and the last they've won since.

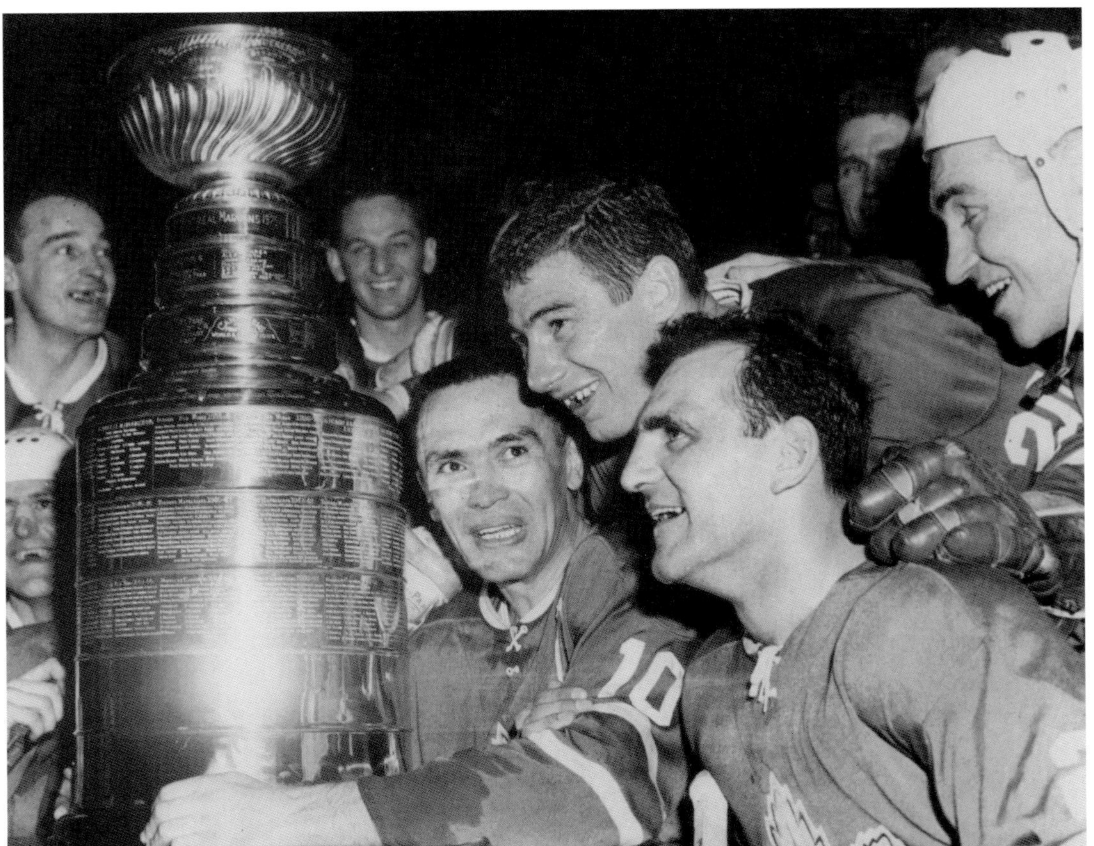

In Toronto's Maple Leafs Gardens dressing room, Leafs coach George "Punch" Imlach pours some bubbly into the 1963 Cup while captain George Armstrong looks on.

Toronto captain George Armstrong and a group of teammates only a dentist—or hockey aficionado—could love celebrate their 1964 Cup win, the team's third in a row.

Jean Beliveau, hockey's smoothest and most elegant player, hoists the 1968 Cup in Montreal Forum. Beliveau would captain two more Cup-winning teams (1969 and 1971) before retiring in 1971 after 20 seasons with Le Club de Hockey Canadien.

Bruins defenseman Bobby Orr hugs goalie Eddie Johnston while teammate Wayne Cashman raises his stick in celebration of Boston's 1972 Stanley Cup win, the teams' second championship in three seasons. Orr scored the Cup-winning goals in 1970 and 1972 and became the first two-time winner of the Conn Smythe Trophy.

Scrappy, yappy Philly captain and sparkplug Bobby Clarke celebrates his team's 1974 Cup win. The brawny Broadway Bullies would also win the Cup in 1975. Fred Shero called Clarke "the perfect captain" and opposing coaches once voted him the player they would most like to have on their team.

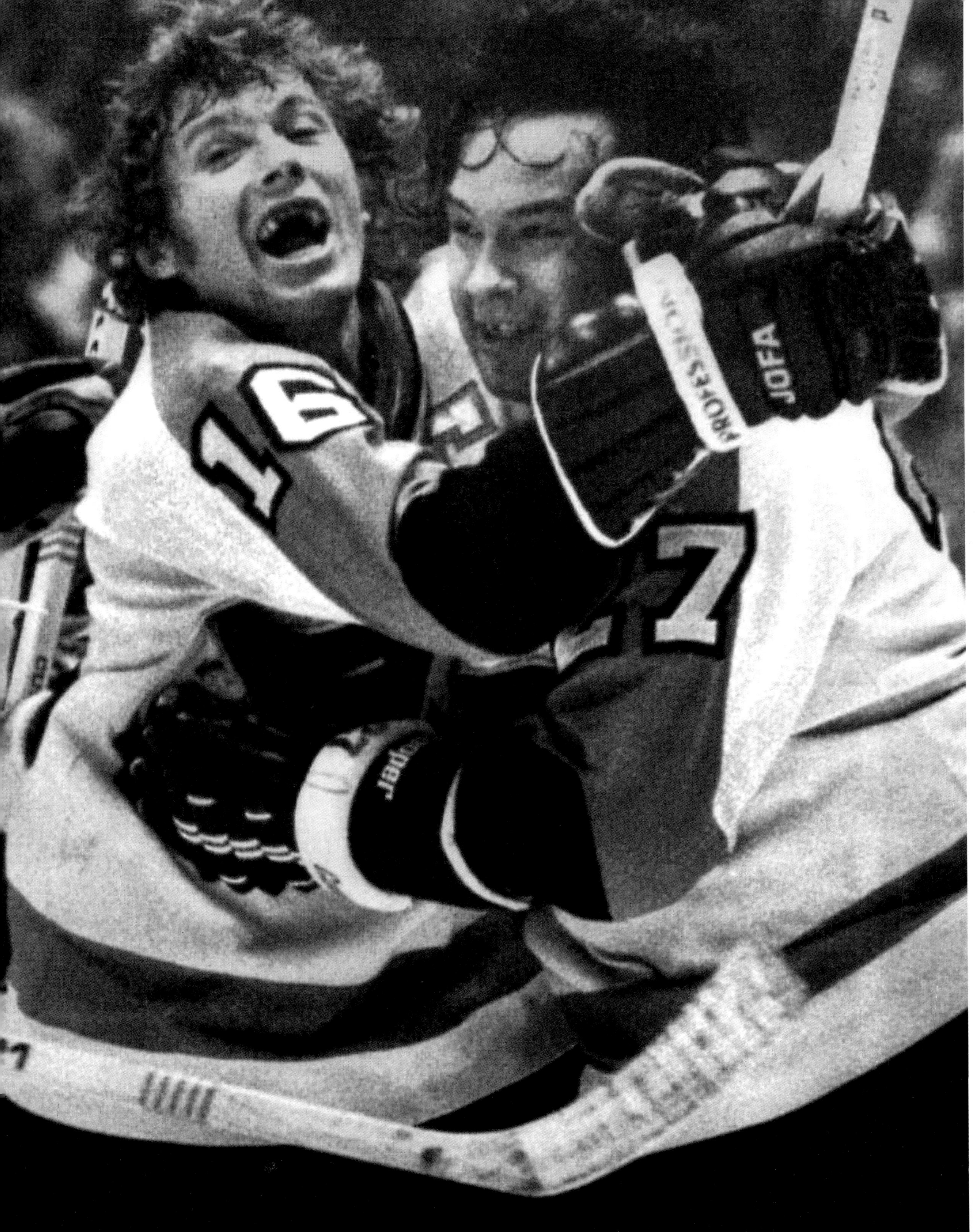
JOFA

Montreal's Rick Chartraw didn't even get his skates off before he popped a cork and cradled the Cup in 1976. This Cup win was the first of four in a row for the dynastic Canadiens.

Montreal's Mario Tremblay swings behind the Boston net after scoring a game winner on Bruins goalie Gerry Cheevers in the Habs' six-game Cup win in 1978.

Bob Gainey, one of the greatest defensive forwards in NHL history, lifts the 1979 Stanley Cup, Montreal's fourth in a row but the first time since 1968 that the Canadiens won the Cup at home.

Islander Butch Goring (white helmet) is set to pounce on goalie Billy Smith as New York defeats Philadelphia for the 1980 Stanley Cup, the first of the Islanders' four in a row

New York Islander defenseman and captain Denis Potvin hoists his and his team's fourth consecutive Cup in 1983 after the veteran Islanders swept the upstart Edmonton Oilers and held Wayne Gretzky goalless.

Wayne Gretzky and the Edmonton Oilers ended one dynasty and launched another when they won the 1984 Stanley Cup from the defending champion New York Islanders. Moments after this photo was taken Gretzky said, "I've won a lot of awards in my life...but nothing compares to this."

Speed killed and thrilled in 1984 as the Edmonton Oilers whirling, up-tempo, Euro-style attack rolled over, around and through the New York Islanders orthodox bump-and-grind defense in five games. "We proved that an offensive team can win the Cup," said Gretzky.

Montreal goalie Patrick Roy was immense in the 1986 finals where his 15-5 record and 1.92 GAA made him, at 20, the youngest player ever to win the Conn Smythe Trophy.

"It's not heavy when you win it; a guy could carry it all day," said Calgary Flames captain Lanny McDonald following his team's six-game win over Montreal in 1989.

Oiler captain Mark Messier, flanked by alternate captains Kevin Lowe (L) and Jari Kurri, lifts the 1990 Stanley Cup, the team's fifth in seven years and first since the 1988 trade of Wayne Gretzky to Los Angeles.

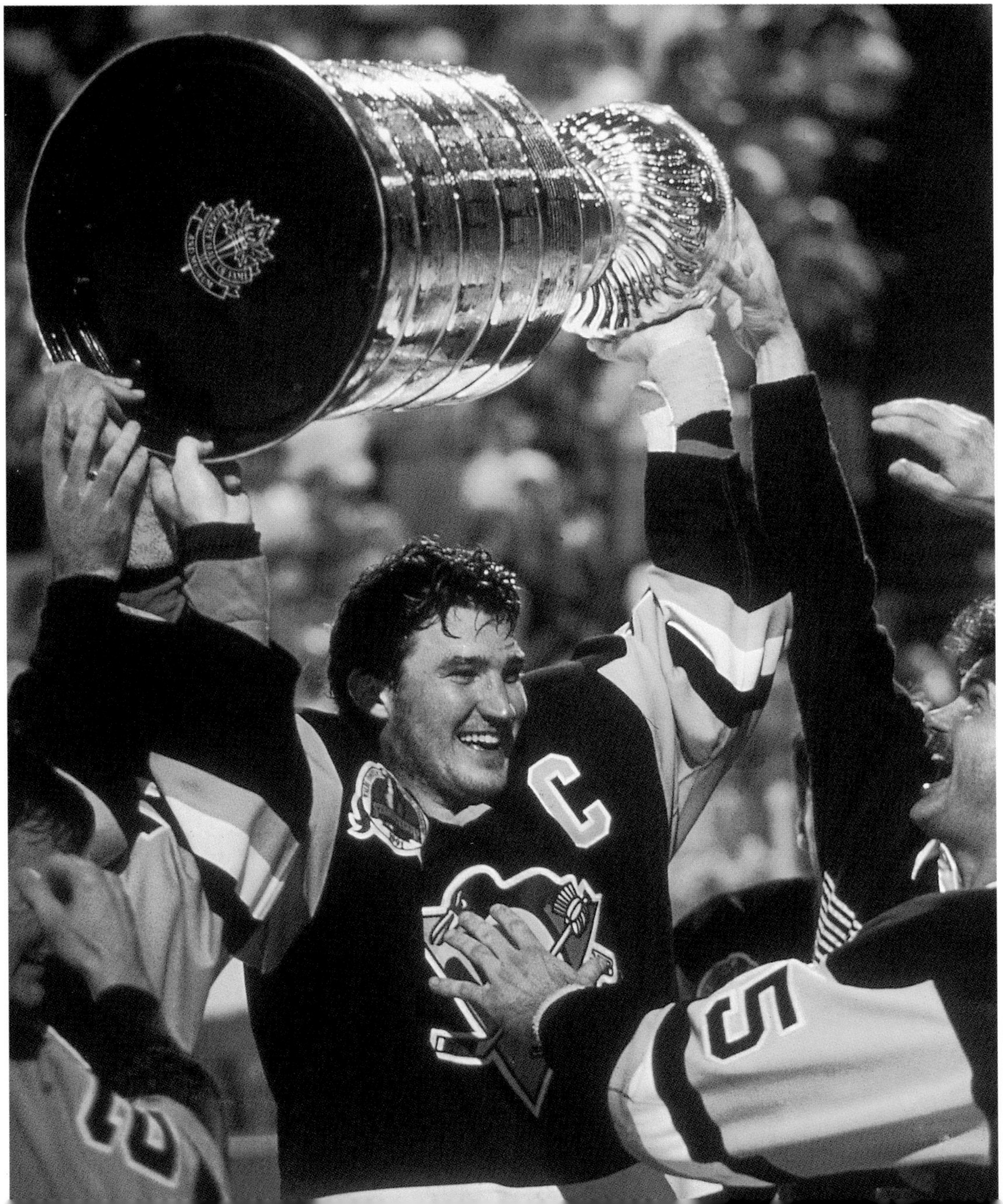

A beaming Mario Lemieux lifts his and Pittsburgh's first Cup in 1991. Despite missing one game of the finals with a bad back, Lemieux's 12 points (five goals) and overall dominating play won him the Conn Smythe Trophy.

RANGERS

In 1994 the New York Rangers finally ended those taunting fan chants of "Nineteen Forty...Nineteen Forty..." by winning the team's first Stanley Cup in 54 years, this in a seven-game series with the Vancouver Canucks that ended with a 3-2 Ranger win in Madison Square Garden.

Colorado captain Joe Sakic and his Avalanche teammates were on a Rocky Mountain high in 1996 when they swept the upstart Florida Panthers to win the Cup in the first year following the franchise's move from Quebec City. Sakic won the Conn Smythe Trophy.

Russian-born Sergei Fedorov shows the 1997 Cup to a jubilant crowd of Red Wings fans at Detroit's Joe Louis Arena. This was Detroit's first Cup win since 1955 and the days of Gordie Howe.

Wheelchair-bound ex-Detroit defenseman Vladimir Konstantinov—almost fatally injured in the crash of a limousine a year earlier—was wheeled onto the ice by teammates after Detroit's 1998 Cup win. Detroit captain Steve Yzerman, who had planned to hand the Cup first to goalie Chris Osgood, impulsively handed it to Konstantinov instead.

Thirty eight years after his father Bobby—the Golden Jet—lifted his first and only Cup with Chicago in 1961, Brett Hull hoisted the same Cup as a member of the 1999 Dallas Stars. "The Golden Brett" scored the controversial Cup-winning goal at 14:51 of the third overtime in Game 6.

"Playoff time is war," New Jersey captain Scott Stevens had said earlier in the 2000 playoffs and shortly after his devastating body check on Philadelphia's Eric Lindros in the Eastern Conference finals. But Stevens—kissing the Cup—looked like a man more interested in love than war following his team's Cup win over Dallas.

2000
STANLEY CUP

Stanley Cup Winners

Since the formation of the NHL in1917

Year	W-L In Finals	Winner	Coach	Finalist	Coach
2001	4-3	Colorado	Bob Hartley	New Jersey	Larry Robinson
2000	4-2	New Jersey	Larry Robinson	Dallas	Ken Hitchcock
1999	4-2	Dallas	Ken Hitchcock	Buffalo	Lindy Ruff
1998	4-0	Detroit	Scotty Bowman	Washington	Ron Wilson
1997	4-0	Detroit	Scotty Bowman	Philadelphia	Terry Murray
1996	4-0	Colorado	Marc Crawford	Florida	Doug MacLean
1995	4-0	New Jersey	Jacques Lemaire	Detroit	Scotty Bowman
1994	4-3	NY Rangers	Mike Keenan	Vancouver	Pat Quinn
1993	4-1	Montreal	Jacques Demers	Los Angeles	Barry Melrose
1992	4-0	Pittsburgh	Scotty Bowman	Chicago	Mike Keenan
1991	4-2	Pittsburgh	Bob Johnson	Minnesota	Bob Gainey
1990	4-1	Edmonton	John Muckler	Boston	Mike Milbury
1989	4-2	Calgary	Terry Crisp	Montreal	Pat Burns
1988	4-0	Edmonton	Glen Sather	Boston	Terry OíReilly
1987	4-3	Edmonton	Glen Sather	Philadelphia	Mike Keenan
1986	4-1	Montreal	Jean Perron	Calgary	Bob Johnson
1985	4-1	Edmonton	Glen Sather	Philadelphia	Mike Keenan
1984	4-1	Edmonton	Glen Sather	NY Islanders	Al Arbour
1983	4-0	NY Islanders	Al Arbour	Edmonton	Glen Sather
1982	4-0	NY Islanders	Al Arbour	Vancouver	Roger Neilson
1981	4-1	NY Islanders	Al Arbour	Minnesota	Glen Sonmor
1980	4-2	NY Islanders	Al Arbour	Philadelphia	Pat Quinn
1979	4-1	Montreal	Scotty Bowman	NY Rangers	Fred Shero
1978	4-2	Montreal	Scotty Bowman	Boston	Don Cherry
1977	4-0	Montreal	Scotty Bowman	Boston	Don Cherry
1976	4-0	Montreal	Scotty Bowman	Philadelphia	Fred Shero
1975	4-2	Philadelphia	Fred Shero	Buffalo	Floyd Smith
1974	4-2	Philadelphia	Fred Shero	Boston	Bep Guidolin
1973	4-2	Montreal	Scotty Bowman	Chicago	Billy Reay
1972	4-2	Boston	Tom Johnson	NY Rangers	Emile Francis
1971	4-3	Montreal	Al MacNeil	Chicago	Billy Reay
1970	4-0	Boston	Harry Sinden	St. Louis	Scotty Bowman
1969	4-0	Montreal	Claude Ruel	St. Louis	Scotty Bowman
1968	4-0	Montreal	Toe Blake	St. Louis	Scotty Bowman
1967	4-2	Toronto	Punch Imlach	Montreal	Toe Blake
1966	4-2	Montreal	Toe Blake	Detroit	Sid Abel
1965	4-3	Montreal	Toe Blake	Chicago	Billy Reay
1964	4-3	Toronto	Punch Imlach	Detroit	Sid Abel
1963	4-1	Toronto	Punch Imlach	Detroit	Sid Abel
1962	4-2	Toronto	Punch Imlach	Chicago	Rudy Pilous
1961	4-2	Chicago	Rudy Pilous	Detroit	Sid Abel
1960	4-3	Montreal	Toe Blake	Toronto	Punch Imlach
1959	4-1	Montreal	Toe Blake	Toronto	Punch Imlach
1958	4-2	Montreal	Toe Blake	Boston	Milt Schmidt
1957	4-1	Montreal	Toe Blake	Boston	Milt Schmidt

Year	*W-L In Finals*	*Winner*	*Coach*	*Finalist*	*Coach*
1956	4-1	Montreal	Toe Blake	Detroit	Jimmy Skinner
1955	4-3	Detroit	Jimmy Skinner	Montreal	Dick Irvin
1954	4-3	Detroit	Tommy Ivan	Montreal	Dick Irvin
1953	4-1	Montreal	Dick Irvin	Boston	Lynn Patrick
1952	4-0	Detroit	Tommy Ivan	Montreal	Dick Irvin
1951	4-1	Toronto	Joe Primeau	Montreal	Dick Irvin
1950	4-3	Detroit	Tommy Ivan	NY Rangers	Lynn Patrick
1949	4-0	Toronto	Hap Day	Detroit	Tommy Ivan
1948	4-0	Toronto	Hap Day	Detroit	Tommy Ivan
1947	4-2	Toronto	Hap Day	Montreal	Dick Irvin
1946	4-1	Montreal	Dick Irvin	Boston	Dit Clapper
1945	4-3	Toronto	Hap Day	Detroit	Jack Adams
1944	4-0	Montreal	Dick Irvin	Chicago	Paul Thompson
1943	4-0	Detroit	Jack Adams	Boston	Art Ross
1942	4-3	Toronto	Hap Day	Detroit	Jack Adams
1941	4-0	Boston	Cooney Weiland	Detroit	Ebbie Goodfellow
1940	4-2	NY Rangers	Frank Boucher	Toronto	Dick Irvin
1939	4-1	Boston	Art Ross	Toronto	Dick Irvin
1938	3-1	Chicago	Bill Stewart	Toronto	Dick Irvin
1937	3-2	Detroit	Jack Adams	NY Rangers	Lester Patrick
1936	3-1	Detroit	Jack Adams	Toronto	Dick Irvin
1935	3-0	Mtl. Maroons	Tommy Gorman	Toronto	Dick Irvin
1934	3-1	Chicago	Tommy Gorman	Detroit	Herbie Lewis
1933	3-1	NY Rangers	Lester Patrick	Toronto	Dick Irvin
1932	3-0	Toronto	Dick Irvin	NY Rangers	Lester Patrick
1931	3-2	Montreal	Cecil Hart	Chicago	Dick Irvin
1930	2-0	Montreal	Cecil Hart	Boston	Art Ross
1929	2-0	Boston	Cy Denneny	NY Rangers	Lester Patrick
1928	3-2	NY Rangers	Lester Patrick	Mtl. Maroons	Eddie Gerard
1927	2-0-2	Ottawa	Dave Gill	Boston	Art Ross
	The National Hockey League assumed control of Stanley Cup competition after 1926				
1926	3-1	Mtl. Maroons	Eddie Gerard	Victoria	
1925	3-1	Victoria	Lester Patrick	Montreal	
1924	2-0	Montreal	Leo Dandurand	Cgy. Tigers	
	2-0			Van. Maroons	
1923	2-0	Ottawa	Pete Green	Edm. Eskimos	
	3-1			Van. Maroons	
1922	3-2	Tor. St. Pats	Eddie Powers	Van. Millionaires	
1921	3-2	Ottawa	Pete Green	Van. Millionaires	
1920	3-2	Ottawa	Pete Green	Seattle	
1919	2-2-1	No decision – series between Montreal and Seattle cancelled due to influenza epidemic			
1918	3-2	Tor. Arenas	Dick Carroll	Van. Millionaires	

Index